WORLD OF WONDERS
A BRAVE NEW WORLD

知の探索

Anthony Sellick

John Barton

Ai Ogasawara

cover photographs by
©iStockphoto
John Barton
Space X
Dcrjsr

photographs by
©iStockphoto
Reuters/AFLO
Jitze Couperus via Flickr
Getty Images
John Barton
Space X
Dcrjsr
Bariston

音声ファイルのダウンロード／ストリーミング

CDマーク表示がある箇所は、音声を弊社HPより無料でダウンロード／ストリーミングすることができます。トップページのバナーをクリックし、書籍検索してください。書籍詳細ページに音声ダウンロードアイコンがございますのでそちらから自習用音声としてご活用ください。

https://www.seibido.co.jp

World of Wonders: A Brave New World

Copyright © 2019 by Anthony Sellick, John Barton, Ai Ogasawara

All rights reserved for Japan.
No part of this book may be reproduced in any form
without permission from Seibido Co., Ltd.

Preface

World of Wonders: A Brave New World is the third in a series of books looking at a variety of important trends that are shaping the modern world. Each of the chapters examines a topic or issue that affects our lives, or which will change our lives in the future. We hope that you will find these topics interesting and thought-provoking. We also hope that they will be sufficiently stimulating to encourage you to learn more about these topics and issues.

The topics covered in the 20 essays range widely and are grouped into four sections: the worlds of culture and society, science and technology, business and economics, and politics and international relations. The topics are drawn from a number of areas ranging from one of the world's favorite toys (Lego), to the importance of taking part in democratic elections. We hope that having read these essays, you will actively seek to develop your own views on the issues raised in this book, and that you will debate them vigorously.

As well as notes in Japanese following each essay, each chapter contains a pre-reading vocabulary exercise and post-reading exercises that are presented to test your comprehension of the essays. There is also a summary exercise for every chapter.

Finally, while we have tried to ensure that the material in this book is up-to-date, due to the fast-changing nature of some of the topics, it is inevitable that by the time the book is published, some things may have changed.

We sincerely hope you enjoy the book.

Anthony Sellick

Contents

The World of Culture and Society

Chapter 1   **Building Blocks, Building Minds**
The Amazing Success of Lego   *1*

Chapter 2   **Faster, Higher, Stronger**
The World's Most Extreme Sports   *7*

Chapter 3   **Do You Hulu?**
The Future of Television   *12*

Chapter 4   **A Woman's Place Is ~~in the Kitchen~~ Wherever She Wants**
Gender Equality   *18*

Chapter 5   **The Internet of Things**
This Changes Everything   *23*

The World of Science and Technology

Chapter 6   **The Supercomputer in Your Pocket**
How Cell Phones Are Changing the World   *29*

Chapter 7   **Land, Sea, and Air**
How Drones Are Changing Our Lives   *34*

Chapter 8   **Forever Young**
The Quest for Eternal Youth   *40*

Chapter 9   **Just Forget It!**
The Science of Rewriting Memories   *45*

Chapter 10   **I Am Who I Am**
Sex, Sexuality, and Gender   *51*

The World of Business and Economics

Chapter 11 **Uber, Airbnb, and TaskRabbit**
Collaborative Consumption and the Sharing Economy   56

Chapter 12 **More Than eMoney**
What Is the Blockchain?   62

Chapter 13 **Permanently Part-Time**
Is the Gig Economy the Future of Work?   68

Chapter 14 **Driven to Succeed**
The Amazing Story of Elon Musk   74

Chapter 15 **The Clanking Masses**
Will a Robot Take Your Job?   80

The World of Politics and International Relations

Chapter 16 **It's None of Your Business!**
Why Privacy Is Important   85

Chapter 17 **I'll See You in Court!**
What Is the Rule of Law?   91

Chapter 18 **Just a Face in the Crowd?**
What Does Equality Really Mean?   96

Chapter 19 **Freedom of the Press Means Freedom of the People**
The Danger of Fake News   101

Chapter 20 **One in a Million**
*Why **Your** Vote Counts*   107

Compiled References by Chapter   113

Chapter 1
Building Blocks, Building Minds
The Amazing Success of Lego

Useful Words

Choose a word from the list below to complete each sentence.

1. After he got his _____, nobody could copy his invention.
2. Losing weight is one _____ of exercise.
3. It is important for companies to _____ and develop new products.
4. Many people create videos and _____ them to YouTube for everyone to watch.
5. He _____ reads books. That is why he is so knowledgeable.

| upload | patent | constantly | innovate | benefit |

Reading

① 02~08

02

1 Have you ever played with Lego? Lego is one of the biggest toy companies in the world and one of the most well-known toy brands. Lego was founded in Denmark in 1932 by Ole Kirk Christiansen. The company originally made high-quality toys from wood. However, in 1958, Ole's son, Godtfred Kirk Christiansen, patented the now famous plastic Lego block. The word Lego is derived from "leg godt," which means "play well," in Danish. It also means "I put together," in Latin. Lego is a special kind of toy that

A young boy displaying his Lego collection and an original spaceship he made himself.

1

can inspire, educate, and entertain both children and adults.

03

2 Lego's simple plastic building blocks encourage people to use their imagination and discover many different ways to play with them. This has become known as the "Lego System of Play," and is the foundation of the huge success of the toy. Many people play with Lego their entire lives — from beginner sets when they are young, through more advanced sets as they get older, to enjoying Lego with their children as adults. In this way, Lego truly spans generations.

04

3 The key to Lego's appeal is simply that children love to play with it. As all Lego blocks fit together, children can constantly make new toys and invent stories involving their creations. As well as being entertaining and encouraging creativity, playing with Lego also has other benefits. Scientists have found that playing with Lego when very young can improve children's ability in math, perceptual skills, and problem-solving. Along with all these benefits, it provides a great connection between children and their parents. This ability of Lego to encourage teamwork and collaboration has been used by psychologists to help children with autism to improve their social skills.

05

4 Lego does not only make toys for children, however. In 1998, the first Lego Mindstorms toys were sold. These Lego toys were for adults and allowed people to build and program robots made from special Lego bricks. In 2004, the first World Robot Olympiad (WRO) — a series of games for robots made using Lego Mindstorms — was held in Singapore with teams from four countries. In the 2016 WRO, held in India, 21,700 teams from 56 countries took part. In the 2016 FIRST LEGO League, a similar competition for elementary and junior high school students, more than 255,000 children in 31,079 teams took part.

06

5 As shown by Lego Mindstorms, one reason behind the continuing success of the Lego brand is its ability to evolve and innovate. In its early years, it switched from making wooden blocks to plastic bricks. At that time, plastic was not often used in toys. The company has also formed tie-ups with other popular brands such as Marvel and Star Wars, allowing fans to build their own versions of those fantasy worlds. But perhaps the most important reason for the continuing success of the Lego brand is that it listens to its customers. Lego Cuusoo is a website that allows Lego fans to upload their designs and vote on other fans' designs. If a design receives more than 10,000 votes, the Lego company will consider creating and selling a set for that design. The first two products created as a result of fans' votes on Lego Cuusoo were the Japanese Shinkai 6500 submersible in 2011 and the Japanese Hayabusa spacecraft in 2012. More recently Lego has introduced products using augmented reality such as the Lego AR Studio. Launched in December 2017, it allows children to combine physical Lego with virtual reality. For example, you can play with a fantasy castle Lego set while a fire-breathing dragon hovers above you! Lego is even used by some companies to develop their businesses, something which is called Lego Serious Play.

6 Like Disney, Lego even has its own theme parks and movies. The first Legoland opened in 1968 in Billund, Denmark. By 2017, there were Legolands in Dubai, England, Germany, Malaysia, Japan, and the United States (in California and Florida). Movies made with Lego, called brickfilms, have been made by fans since the early 1970s, and it is easy to find many brickfilms on Internet sites such as YouTube. The Lego company encourages this, and between 2000 and 2003, released several Lego Studios sets for movie makers. In 2014, the first Hollywood Lego movie, called *The Lego Movie*, was released. It was a huge success, making $469 million. Since then several more successful Lego movies have been made.

The eighth Legoland opened in Nagoya, Japan on April 1, 2017.

7 Today, Lego continues to be a powerful force in the toy world and beyond. Its mission "To inspire and develop the builders of tomorrow," is still as relevant, powerful, and as fun as ever. Lego will undoubtedly continue to inspire future generations. As Kjeld Kirk Kristiansen, the grandson of the founder said, "We are all growing older all the time, but we don't need to grow up. There'll always be a child inside and the child wants to have fun."

NOTES

Ole Kirk Christiansen「オーレ・キアク・クリスチャンセン（1891-1958）」デンマークの玩具メーカー LEGO®（レゴ®）の創業者。Godtfred（ゴッドフレッド；1920-1995）は三男、Kjeld（ケル；1947-）は孫。　**Latin**「ラテン語」　**key to ~**「～を理解する鍵（ポイント）」　**perceptual skill**「知覚能力」　**autism**「自閉症」　**social skill**「社会的交流能力」対人関係における挨拶、交渉、自己主張などの技能。社会的スキル。　**World Robot Olympiad (WRO)**「ワールド・ロボット・オリンピアード（WRO）」小中高生によるロボット競技の国際大会で、毎年開催される。ロボット製作とプログラム開発のトータル技術で競う自律型ロボットのコンテスト。　**FIRST LEGO League**「ファースト・レゴ・リーグ」米国の NPO 法人「FIRST」とレゴ社が運営する国際的なロボット競技会。**Marvel** マーベル・コミックス社がその前々身の出版社名で発刊した漫画雑誌『マーベル・コミックス』(*Marvel Comics*)(1939 ～)。ここから生まれたヒーローたちはその後映画化もされ、現在もコミックスと映画の双方で米国のエンターテインメント業界をリードしている。これらのヒーローたちを総称して "マーベルの" スーパーヒーローと呼ぶ。マーベル・コミックスおよび現在の親会社であるマーベル・エンターテインメントは、キャプテン・アメリカやスパイダーマンなど超人的な力で知られる米国のスーパーヒーローのほとんどを生み出した。　**Star Wars** ジョージ・ルーカス監督によって世界観が生み出され製作された宇宙映画シリーズ。1977 年にシリーズ最初の作品『スター・ウォーズ』(*Star Wars*) が公開。後に『スター・ウォーズ　エピソード４：新たなる希望』(*Star Wars: Episode IV—A New Hope*)に改題されている。2015 年のエピソード７からウォルト・ディズニー社が製作している。**Lego Cuusoo** 2008 ～ 14 年に運営されたウェブサイトで、後継サイトは Lego Ideas。　**vote on ~**「～に（ついて）投票する」　**Shinkai 6500**「しんかい 6500」日本の海洋研究開発機構が開発した有人潜水調査船。乗組員は 3 人で、6,500 メートルの深海まで潜行可能。　**submersible**「潜水艇，潜水調査船」　**Hayabusa**「はやぶさ」日本の宇宙航空研究開発機構（JAXA）が 2003 年に打ち上げた小惑星探査機。2005 年に小惑星「イトカワ」に着地して砂粒を採取、2010 年に砂粒の入った耐熱カプセルを地球に届けた。はやぶさ自身は大気圏突入で燃え尽きた。　**augmented reality**「拡張現実」実世界から得られる知覚情報にコンピューターで生み出される情報を重ね合わせ、人の知覚体験を豊かにする技術。　**virtual reality**「仮想現実」　**Lego Serious Play**「レゴ・シリアスプレイ」レゴ社が開発した組織活性化の手法。レゴブロックを用いて参加者が心の内面をブロックで立体化・可視化させ、問題解決やチームビルディング、組織のビジョンづくりなどへ導くワークショップ形式のビジネス研修。　**Billund**「ビルン」デンマークのユトランド半島中央部の町で、レゴ本社もある。**Dubai**「ドバイ」アラブ首長国連邦を構成する 7 首長国の 1 つ。アラビア半島南東部のペルシャ湾の出口に位置する。首都はドバイ市。　**brickfilm**「ブリックフィルム」レゴブロックなどのプラスチック製ブロック玩具を使用して制作されたコマ撮りアニメーション映画。日本語のレゴブロックは、英語では Lego brick と呼ばれている。brick は「煉瓦（れんが）」の意。

Questions for Understanding

Part 1 *Look at the following statements. Write T if the statement is true, and F if it is false. Write the number of the paragraph where you find the answer in the parenthesis.*

1. Since it began, Lego has made its toys from plastic.

T/F

(#　　　)

2. Lego is popular both with children and adults.

T/F

(#　　　)

Chapter 1   **Building Blocks, Building Minds** – *The Amazing Success of Lego*

3. Playing with Lego can help children to become inventors.

T/F

(#   )

4. Lego allows its customers to decide new designs via an online system.

T/F

(#   )

Part 2   *Look at the questions below. Check the best answer for each.*

1. What is the main reason that Lego is popular?
   a. ☐ Lego is very good at marketing.
   b. ☐ Lego helps children to do well at school.
   c. ☐ Lego is enjoyed by children.
   d. ☐ Lego teaches people about new technology.

2. When will Lego decide to manufacture a Lego set on Cuusoo?
   a. ☐ When it is confirmed that there will be a tie-up with a big brand
   b. ☐ When the number of customer votes reaches a certain number
   c. ☐ When a large number of customers write to the company suggesting a certain model
   d. ☐ When children testing the models confirm it is popular

3. Why was the first Hollywood Lego movie made?
   a. ☐ Because Disney suggested a partnership deal
   b. ☐ Because many Lego fans told the company they wanted to see one
   c. ☐ Because the brickfilms suggested that there was a demand for an official movie
   d. ☐ Because a movie studio was created at Legoland in Denmark

4. What does Kjeld Kirk Kristiansen mean by his statement "We are all growing older all the time, but we don't need to grow up."?
   a. ☐ Lego is still popular among children of all ages
   b. ☐ Lego is trying to increase its popularity among adults
   c. ☐ Lego reminds us it is important to maintain a childlike curiosity in life
   d. ☐ Lego helps older people to relate to younger people

5

Summary

Fill each space with the best word or phrase from the list below.

> enhance   relevant   evolve   Olympiad   derived from   put together

The word Lego is 1) _____ the Danish words "leg godt" which means "play well," and the company has delighted children and adults for generations. Lego blocks can be 2) _____ in an endless number of ways, which fires the imaginations of those playing with them. One key to Lego's success is its ability to 3) _____ and keep offering new sets to play with. Another is to incorporate new technology into their "system of play." In 2004, a robot 4) _____ was held in Singapore, in which all the robots were made from Lego Mindstorms sets. Lego's success seems assured as it continues to 5) _____ its products in order to remain 6) _____ to new generations of customers.

What do YOU think?

Choose ONE of the statements below. Do you agree or disagree with it? Why? Prepare a short response giving your opinion.

> ▶ Lego is the best toy in the world.
> ▶ If you don't encourage your children to play with Lego, you are a bad parent.

....
....
....
....

> *You can discover more about a person in an hour of play than in a year of conversation.*
>
> Plato (428/427 - 348/347 BCE)
> Ancient Greek philosopher

Chapter 2

Faster, Higher, Stronger

The World's Most Extreme Sports

Useful Words

Choose a word or phrase from the list below to complete each sentence.

1. Jesse Owens was the first _____ to win four gold medals during the Olympic Games.

2. In 2016, Germany welcomed nearly 1 million _____ who had escaped the war in Syria.

3. Many people are surprised to discover that the pineapple _____ in South America.

4. This class _____ of students from Japan, China, Korea, Brazil, Peru, and Guam.

5. He did not want to _____ in the student council because he was too shy.

| (be) made up | refugees | originated | take part | athlete |

Reading

1 The motto of the Olympic Games is Citius, Altius, Fortius, which means, "Faster, Higher, Stronger." The Olympic Games are the world's largest sporting event. In the 2016 Summer Olympic Games in Rio de Janeiro, more than 11,000 athletes from 204 countries and territories, plus an additional team made of refugees, participated. Between August 5 and August 21, 2016, these athletes competed in 306 different sporting events. However, even the Olympic Games cannot include every sport enjoyed around the world. Yet, despite this, these sports also embody the Olympic motto. Let's find out about some of them.

7

2 *Indoor Skydiving*: When we think of skydiving, we usually imagine leaping out of an airplane high in the sky and drifting down to earth under a parachute. But what do you do when the weather is bad? The answer is to practice indoors using a vertical wind tunnel. This is an enormous fan that generates winds as fast as 230 kilometers per hour. Indoor skydiving developed from this kind of practice. Because they use a vertical wind tunnel, no parachutes are needed, and the competitors can literally dance on air as they perform individually choreographed routines suspended in the air, or race to complete a set routine as fast as possible. At the 2017 Windoor Wind Games held in Catalonia in Spain, 14-year-old Kyra Poh from Singapore won gold medals for the solo freestyle and solo speed events.

These Singaporean girls enjoy floating on air in 2012.

3 *Ultramarathons*: The marathon is the culmination of the Summer Olympic Games, a 42.195-kilometer run in the summer sun. However, some people are not satisfied with running a marathon and want to go further. Ultramarathons are running races that have distances of 50 kilometers, 100 kilometers, or even more. Most, like marathons, are run on tracks or along roads, but some are off-road. For example, the 4 Deserts Race Series is an annual event consisting of four 250-kilometer races across deserts in China, Chile, Africa, and finally in Antarctica. Since it began in 2002, more than 8,000 people have taken part. Perhaps the greatest runner of them all is Serge Girard from France, who has run from coast to coast across the continents of Africa, Australia, Eurasia, North America, and South America. In 2009 and 2010, he ran for 365 days and covered a distance of 27,011 kilometers.

4 *Iron Men and Wife Carrying*: Some people get bored just running for a long time. If they want some company, perhaps they could try wife carrying. Wife carrying contests originated in Finland in 1992, based on a folk tale about a wife-stealing bandit. In the contest, men carry their wives (or their neighbor's wife) over a 253.5-meter course which includes sand traps and a pool of water. The champion wins his wife's weight in beer! A more serious competition is the Ironman Triathlon, which is made up of a 3.86-kilometer swim, followed by a 180.25-kilometer bicycle ride, and completed with a 42.2-kilometer run, all of which must be completed within 17 hours. The first race took place in 1977 as the result of an argument over whether swimmers, cyclists, or runners were the fittest, and since then, thousands of people have competed to become an Ironman. Although competitors have 17 hours to complete the event, the record times are much less than that. The current men's record was set by Australian Craig Alexander in 2011, with a time of 8 hours, 3 minutes, and 56 seconds. The current women's record was set in 2016 by Daniela Ryf from Switzerland. Her time was 8 hours, 46 minutes, and 46 seconds

5 *Mud Running*: If being an Ironman does not appeal to you, and wife carrying just seems too silly (or if you are single), then perhaps you could try the Tough Mudder race. This event involves running 16-19 kilometers along a muddy, cross-country course full of obstacles. Most events have between 20 and 25 obstacles, but every event includes four particular

How far can YOU run?

obstacles: Arctic Enema (a dip into ice-cold water), Electroshock Therapy (a field of mud covered with wires hanging over it that give 10,000-volt shocks), Funky Monkey (slippery monkey bars over an ice-cold pool of water), and Everest (running up a slippery quarter pipe — the kind of ramp used by skateboarders). Since it began in 2010, more than 2.5 million people have taken part in Tough Mudder races around the world.

6 None of the above events are likely to appear in the Olympic Games, but they show that millions of people around the world are inspired by the Olympic motto, "faster, higher, stronger." But why do people put themselves through such grueling events? Researchers at Cardiff University in Britain tried to find out. They found that taking part in such tough and painful events helped people to feel more fulfilled and to forget about the stresses of everyday life. The growing popularity of extreme sports shows that many people are seeking ways to take control of their bodies and their lives, as well as to be able to cast themselves as the heroes in their own life stories. *Citius, Altius, Fortius*.

NOTES

motto「モットー，標語」 **territory**「政治的支配下にある領土」 "countries and territories" は日本語で通常「国と地域」と表記される。 **embody**「（思想や感情を）具体的に表現する・体現する」 **indoor skydiving**「インドア・スカイダイビング」下方からの強烈な風に吹き上げられながら空中に浮遊し、表現力や回転などの技を競う。 **leap out of ~**「～から飛び出す・跳び出す」 **vertical wind tunnel**「垂直風洞」垂直のトンネル型装置で、下から強烈な風が吹き上がる。 **literally**「文字通り」 **choreographed**「振り付けされた」 **Catalonia**「カタルーニャ自治州」スペイン北東端のフランスおよび地中海に接する自治州。 **Windoor Wind Games**「ウィンドア・ウインドゲームズ」ウィンドアが主催するインドア・スカイダイビングの世界大会。2018 年で 5 回目の大会。 **culmination of ~**「～で最も盛り上がるもの；～の最高潮」 **originate in ~**「～に始まる；～に由来する」 **folk tale**「民話」 **sand trap**「サンドトラップ」砂場状の障害。ゴルフ競技では「バンカー」と呼ばれるもの。 **argument over ~**「～に関する論争」 **the fittest**「適者，鉄人」 **obstacle**「障害物」 **monkey bars**「雲梯（うんてい）」水平または弧状に作られたはしご状のものにぶら下がり、交互に手を替えながら遊んでいく遊具。 **quarter pipe**「クオーターパイプ」パイプ（管）の断面の 4 分の 1 の「ノ」の字型をした傾斜面のコース。 **ramp**「傾斜面」 **grueling**「へとへとに疲れる」 **put ~ through** …「～に…を受けさせる・経験させる」 **cast ~ as the hero**「～にヒーローの役を与える」

Questions for Understanding

Part 1 *Look at the following statements. Write T if the statement is true, and F if it is false. Write the number of the paragraph where you find the answer in the parenthesis.*

1. Every sport played in the world is included in the Olympic Games.

   T/F (#)

2. Unlike regular skydivers, indoor skydivers do not need a parachute.

   T/F (#)

3. Because it is off-road, the 4 Deserts Race Series is not an ultramarathon.

   T/F (#)

4. Scientists have found that taking part in these events increases stress.

   T/F (#)

Part 2 *Look at the questions below. Check the best answer for each.*

1. How many teams took part in the 2016 Olympic Games?
   a. ☐ 204   b. ☐ 205   c. ☐ 306   d. ☐ 11,000

2. Which continent has Serge Girard *not* run across?
   a. ☐ Africa   b. ☐ Americas   c. ☐ Antarctica   d. ☐ Australia

Chapter 2   **Faster, Higher, Stronger** – *The World's Most Extreme Sports*

3. Why was the Ironman Triathlon started?
    a. ☐ To discover what kind of athlete was the fittest
    b. ☐ To discover whether men or women were fitter
    c. ☐ Because of a folk tale about a wife-stealing bandit
    d. ☐ Because people wanted to win a lot of beer

4. How many obstacles are in every Tough Mudder race?
    a. ☐ 4   b. ☐ 16-19   c. ☐ 20   d. ☐ 25

Summary

① 16

Fill each space with the best word or phrase from the list below.

| be completed   vertical   appeal to   obstacles   consist of   feel fulfilled |

How would you like to run 250 kilometers across a desert? Perhaps you would like to try running along a muddy course filled with 1) _____ that freeze and shock you. Does dancing on air in a 2) _____ wind tunnel 3) _____ you? Extreme sports 4) _____ events that can only 5) _____ if people push themselves to their limits. Why would anyone do this kind of thing for fun? The reason is that just taking part helps the participants to 6) _____, and helps them to feel in control of their bodies and lives.

What do YOU think?

Choose ONE of the statements below. Do you agree or disagree with it? Why? Prepare a short response giving your opinion.

▶ I want to try an extreme sport.
▶ I do not think it is important to do sports or exercise.

....

....

Try again. Fail again. Fail better.

Samuel Becket (1906-89)
Irish author

11

Chapter 3

Do You Hulu?

The Future of Television

Useful Words

Choose a word from the list below to complete each sentence.

1. A _____ that is very widely used is the smartphone.
2. _____ TV services such as Hulu and Netflix are very popular these days.
3. Many people _____ to a daily newspaper.
4. Many animal species are under _____ around the world.
5. Due to one _____ after another, he could not get his report finished on time.

| interruption | subscribe | threat | streaming | device |

Reading

① 17~22

17

1 Television has occupied a very important place in millions of people's lives. Many families have gathered around the screen to watch the defining moments of their age. The moon
5 landing of 1969 still ranks as one of the most watched TV moments of all time. Most of us have grown up watching TV and we often got most of our information and
10 entertainment from it. Today, the role of TV in our lives is undergoing

An illustration of the variety of devices that we can use to watch our favorite content these days.

significant change because of new and improving technologies. There is now a wide choice of devices on which to view content, such as tablets, smartphones, and devices like Apple TV and Google Chromecast. The difference between TV, computers, and the Internet is becoming blurred.

2 What we watch is also undergoing quite a change. In the past, national TV networks such as the BBC in the United Kingdom, NHK in Japan, and ABC and NBC in the United States decided what we would watch. These big networks made money from annual license fees, advertising, and subscription fees. However, Internet-based services are offering serious competition to these traditional networks. This is possible because Internet speeds have significantly improved, enabling the streaming of high-quality video. For example, between 2007 and 2017, the average Internet connection speed in the U.S. rose from 3.67 Mbps to 18.75 Mbps, a fivefold increase in just 10 years. In Japan, the average Internet connection speed in 2017 was even faster, at 20.2 Mbps.

3 Netflix is perhaps the global market leader for streaming TV services, with over 120 million subscribers worldwide. Netflix was founded in 1997 and is now available in more than 190 countries. Another very large provider is Hulu, which has 12 million subscribers in Canada, Japan, and the U.S. To use Netflix or Hulu, you only need an Internet connection and an appropriate device.

Netflix and Hulu have emerged as the dominant players in the streaming TV business in recent years.

There is no need for a decoding box, a satellite dish, or any additional cabling. In addition, the cost and commitment are very low compared to traditional cable TV services. Netflix and Hulu cost about $10 a month and you can quit and sign up again at your convenience. There are no long-term contracts or penalty clauses. Furthermore, you can watch programs and movies whenever you want with no interruptions from advertising. For these reasons, many people are quitting their cable TV contracts and changing to streaming services. They are sometimes called "cord cutters."

20 🎧

5   **4** Streaming companies also make programs and movies that can only be watched by their subscribers. Netflix has created several award-winning series, movies, and documentaries including *Stranger Things*, *Mudbound*, and *Icarus*. Hulu, which has been making original content since 2011, has also created award-winning series, such as *The Handmaid's Tale*. The desire to watch these programs encourages

10   people to subscribe to their services.

21 🎧

5 However, while they are under threat, we should not write off traditional TV networks just yet. Live sports, one of the most viewed categories of program around the world, can usually only be seen on traditional TV networks. One reason for this is the enormous cost. For example, in the U.K., it costs TV networks more than $7

15   billion to broadcast one year of Premier League soccer games. Likewise, in the U.S., Disney's ESPN and WarnerMedia's TNT will pay a combined total of $24 billion over nine years to broadcast NBA basketball games. As these sporting events are watched by millions or even billions of people (for events like the Olympic Games or the soccer World Cup), companies are willing to pay so much money because they

20   can also earn huge amounts from advertising. Perhaps fortunately for the traditional networks, Netflix has said that it is not interested in broadcasting live sports since such programming does not fit the company's business model.

22 🎧

6 While Hulu, Netflix, and others are disrupting the TV business today, it is unclear what the final result will be. From newspapers and books to the radio,

25   to movies, to TV, to computer games, and now to Internet streaming, the history of media is that of one generation's favorite media being replaced by the next generation's preference. However, we still have, use, and enjoy all of those different kinds of media. It may be that Hulu and Netflix will become the preferred media of a generation only to be replaced by some other kind of media in their turn.

Chapter 3　　**Do You Hulu?** – *The Future of Television*

NOTES

defining moment「決定的瞬間」　**Apple TV**「アップル TV」アップル社の製品（iPhone, iPad, Mac コンピューター）の画面をテレビに表示させたり、動画や音楽をテレビ画面に出力するなどして楽しむための機器。　**Google Chromecast**「グーグル・クロームキャスト」グーグルが開発・販売する小型の機器。テレビの HDMI 端子につないで使用する。ユーチューブなどにアップロードされている動画や、インターネット上のウェブサイトなどをテレビ画面で楽しむことができる。　**become blurred**「ぼやける，曖昧になる」　**subscription fee**「受信料，購読料」**streaming** (n)「ストリーミング」通信回線で送受信される動画などのデータをリアルタイムで再生する技術、また再生すること。　**Mbps** (= megabits per second)「メガビット／秒；メガビット毎秒」データ通信速度の単位の1つで、1秒間に 100 万ビットのデータを送れる単位。約 12 万文字の英文字を送信する速度、約 6 万文字の日本語を送信する速度。　**decoding box**「データ復号器」通常「セット・トップ・ボックス (set-top box)(STB)」と呼ばれ、ケーブルテレビのケーブルと受像機を接続する機器。ケーブルテレビなどを一般のテレビで視聴可能な信号へ変換する装置。テレビセットの上に置いたことからこう呼ばれる。　**commitment**「（契約上の）義務」従来のケーブルテレビの利用サービスでは、例えばあらかじめ 1 年分の利用料を支払えば必要な機器を無料で取り付ける、といった契約が用意されていることがあった。　**sign up**「契約する；加入する」　**contract**「契約」**penalty clause**「違反条項」例えば 1 年契約をして 6 カ月で退会を申し出た場合に違約金を支払う必要があるなどの契約違反に関する契約書の記述。　**cord cutter**「ケーブルテレビの契約を解約する人」　***Stranger Things***『ストレンジャー・シングス　未知の世界』（2016 年〜）ネットフリックス製作の SF ホラーのテレビドラマシリーズ。1980 年代の有名映画などへのオマージュ（酷似したシーンの再現）が満載されている。　***Mudbound***『マッドバウンド哀しき友情』（2017）ネットフリックス製作の映画作品。第 90 回（2018 年）アカデミー賞で助演女優賞、脚色賞、撮影賞など 4 部門にノミネートされた。　***Icarus***『イカロス』（2017）ネットフリックス製作のドキュメンタリー作品。ロシアの国家主導によるドーピング計画など、スポーツ界におけるドーピング問題に迫った作品。第 90 回アカデミー賞で長編ドキュメンタリー賞を受賞。　***The Handmaid's Tale***『ハンドメイズ・テイル／侍女の物語』第 70 回（2018 年）エミー賞ドラマ部門作品賞、主演女優賞他計 15 部門 20 項目でノミネートされた。原作はカナダの作家マーガレット・アトウッド (Margaret Atwood) の同名のディストピア小説（1985）。　**under threat**「危機に瀕して」　**write off**「見限る；無用なものとみなす」　**Premier League**「プレミアリーグ」英国・イングランドのプロサッカーの最上位リーグ。　**Disney's ESPN** ESPN は米国のテレビ局。スポーツ専門チャンネルで、国内最大のケーブルテレビ網。1979 年放送開始。現在はウォルト・ディズニー社の傘下。　**Time Warner's TNT** 米メディア大手タイム・ワーナー傘下のケーブルテレビ網。ターナー・ネットワーク・テレビジョン（Turner Network Television）の略。　**a combined total of ~**「総計で〜」　**NBA** (= National Basketball Association)「米プロバスケットボール協会」　**disrupt**「混乱させる」

Questions for Understanding

Part 1 *Look at the following statements. Write T if the statement is true, and F if it is false. Write the number of the paragraph where you find the answer in the parenthesis.*

1. Television has lost its dominant role in our lives.

   T/F ____
   (#   )

2. Internet connection speeds have increased tenfold in the last five years.

   T/F ____
   (#   )

3. Netflix is the biggest provider of streaming services over the Internet.

   T/F ____
   (#   )

4. Netflix has stated that it does not have the money to bid for big sports broadcasting contracts.

   T/F ____
   (#   )

Part 2 *Look at the questions below. Check the best answer for each.*

1. According to the passage, why was 1969 important?
   a. ☐ It was the year that TV services became available all over the world.
   b. ☐ The possibilities of Internet TV were revealed for the first time.
   c. ☐ The moon landing became one of the most watched TV events ever.
   d. ☐ The moon landing was watched by many families for the first time.

2. What are the attractions of services such as Hulu and Netflix?
   a. ☐ They are cheaper and more convenient than traditional TV.
   b. ☐ The picture quality is better than traditional TV.
   c. ☐ You can sign up for a one-year contract and watch as many programs as you like.
   d. ☐ You can get a free cord-cutting service.

3. What is *not* an example of content made by streaming services?
   a. ☐ TV series
   b. ☐ Documentaries
   c. ☐ Movies
   d. ☐ Sporting events

4. Why can traditional TV networks maintain a large position in the industry?
   a. ☐ They still broadcast very popular programs.
   b. ☐ Most people still prefer the TV as a viewing device.
   c. ☐ Watching TV via a broadcast or a cable service is still the cheapest option.
   d. ☐ Large networks have large marketing budgets.

16

Chapter 3   **Do You Hulu?** – *The Future of Television*

Summary

① 23

Fill each space with the best word from the list below.

blurred	undergoing	significantly	disrupting	preferences	enormous

Like so many other areas of our lives, the TV and broadcasting industry is 1) _____ a great deal of change. The availability of multiple devices and the arrival of streaming services are 2) _____ the traditional way of doing things. In addition, Internet connection speeds have increased 3) _____. The TV networks are still in business though as they are able to pay the 4) _____ sums required to buy the rights to broadcast large sporting events. We can expect further changes as boundaries become increasingly 5) _____ and 6) _____ shift as generations change along with the way they consume media.

What do YOU think?

Choose ONE of the statements below. Do you agree or disagree with it? Why? Prepare a short response giving your opinion.

▶ I can watch anything for free on the Internet.
▶ Even with many new technologies and services, traditional TV networks will survive.

....

....

....

....

> *You don't have to turn on the TV set. You don't have to work on the Internet. It's up to you.*
>
> Ray Bradbury (1920-2012)
> American author

17

Chapter 4

A Woman's Place Is ~~in the Kitchen~~ Wherever She Wants

Gender Equality

Useful Words

Choose a word or phrase from the list below to complete each sentence.

1. She is so _____ she never asks anyone for help.

2. If you have never played baseball before, you _____ strike out quickly.

3. Changing your hairstyle or growing a beard can completely change your _____.

4. He turned off his phone so that he could _____ studying for the test.

5. _____ the bad weather, he managed to finish the race with a good time.

appearance	self-reliant	despite	focus on	(be) likely to

Reading

① 24~31

24

1 On Friday, October 24, 1975, 90 percent of the women of Iceland did not go to work nor did they do any cleaning, washing, shopping, or childcare. Why did they go on strike like this? The reason was that they wanted to demonstrate how important their work was for the country and that they had had enough of men
5 controlling their lives.

25

2 It is often said that men are from Mars and women are from Venus, meaning that men and women are very different. In many cultures, being a man means being tough, ambitious, dominant, self-reliant, messy, interested in sports, and focused on their careers, while being a woman means being shy, submissive, organized, clean,

18

interested in children, and focused on their appearance. But what differences has science found?

3 The most obvious difference between men and women is that women can give birth to babies while men cannot. As children, girls are more likely to play with dolls and play social games, while boys are more likely to play with toy weapons and play competitive games. But during their childhood, all children play all kinds of games with all kinds of toys.

Shouldn't they all have the same opportunities?

As our bodies become more adult, women develop wider hips and men develop wider shoulders. This means that, while the average woman can safely give birth, she will run about 10 percent slower than the average man, and will not be as physically strong. Despite decades of studies, no real mental differences between men and women have been found. In other words, none of the cultural ideas of what being a man or woman means are supported by science. But even if there were large differences between the average man and the average woman, would it really matter? After all, are you average in everything? Consider Hiromi Miyake, for example. At 48 kg, she is below the average weight of a Japanese woman (about 50.5 kg), but she can lift far more than average (108 kg), and won a silver medal at the 2012 London Olympics and a bronze medal at the 2016 Rio Olympics.

4 And yet, despite there being very little real difference between men and women, for thousands of years women have been treated very differently from men. Women have been prevented from owning property, choosing who they would marry, voting, getting an education, and working. Even if women were allowed to work, they were often limited in the kinds of jobs they could do, and they were always paid less than men. In other words, for much of history, women were not citizens — they were property.

5 In the mid-19th century, some women began campaigning to be given the same rights in society as men. They faced great opposition from their governments, religious organizations, and even from many women. The early feminists simply wanted men and women to have the same opportunities in life, but for this many were sent to prison, and some even lost their lives. However, they did not give up, and slowly things began to change.

6 After nearly 200 years of campaigning, the position of women in society in most countries has improved greatly, but many women still face incredible difficulties. For example, in Ethiopia and Ghana in Africa, and Bangladesh in southern Asia, nearly one in three girls are married to a man chosen by their parents before they are 15 years old. In Saudi Arabia, women need a letter written by their father or husband before they can get a job. Even in Hollywood, male actors are paid more than female actors. In 2016, the highest paid female actor earned less money than the top five male actors.

7 However, while gender inequality mostly affects the lives of women, it also has an impact on men. For example, when society expects men to be tough and self-reliant, they are less likely to visit a doctor when they feel ill, or to ask for help when they have emotional problems. It should be no surprise that women live five years longer than men on average, nor that the leading cause of death for young men is suicide. If that were not enough, the OECD estimates that the cost to the global economy of treating men and women differently is nearly $12 trillion. The goal of many feminists is to solve these problems for both men and women. If you believe that men and women should have the same opportunities and rights, you are a feminist. If you do not, then you are part of the problem.

8 The 1975 strike resulted in many changes in Iceland. Today, half of the politicians in the government are women, companies are required to pay men and women equally, and large companies must ensure that at least 40 percent of their directors are women. The women of Iceland still strike, but each year they start the strike later in the working day to represent their progress. In 2016, the strike began at 2:38 p.m. A lot of progress has been made, but there is still more for all of us to do.

Isn't this obvious?

NOTES

gender inequality「（社会的・文化的に形成された）性差による不平等」　**Iceland**「アイスランド」北大西洋北部で北極圏に接する世界最北の島国　**have had enough of ~**「~にはうんざりだ」　**Mars**「火星」　**Venus**「金星」　**more likely to ~**「~する傾向が強い」　**social**

Chapter 4　**A Woman's Place Is ~~in the Kitchen~~ Wherever She Wants** — *Gender Equality*

game 一緒に行う仲間と協力しながら進めていくようなゲームや遊び。社会性や協調性を育むと考えられている。　**competitive game** 参加する仲間と点数や速さ、距離などを競い合いながら進めていく種類のゲームや遊び。　**after all**「（前文への証拠・理由・補足・説明を示して）そもそも；だって～だから」　**and yet**「それなのに；それにもかかわらず」　**feminist**「男女同権主義者，女性解放論者」　**have an impact on ~**「～に影響を与える」　**emotional problem**「情緒面の問題」　**If that were not enough**「もしもそれ（＝前文で示した例）では十分でないならば」　**OECD** (= Organization for Economic Cooperation and Development)「経済協力開発機構」先進国間の意見交換や情報交換を通して経済成長、貿易自由化、途上国支援に貢献することを目的とする国際機構。1961 年発足、本部はパリ。　**cost to ~**「～にかかるコスト；～に与える負担」　**director**「（会社の）重役，取締役」

Questions for Understanding

Part 1　*Look at the following statements. Write T if the statement is true, and F if it is false. Write the number of the paragraph where you find the answer in the parenthesis.*

1. According to the passage, October 24 is a national holiday in Iceland.

   T/F
   (#　　　)

2. The passage informs us that men and women think in very different ways.

   T/F
   (#　　　)

3. The passage states that gender inequality is bad for both men and women.

   T/F
   (#　　　)

4. According to the passage, gender equality is an ongoing process.

   T/F
   (#　　　)

Part 2　*Look at the questions below. Check the best answer for each.*

1. Choose the word that has the closest meaning to "incredible" in the following sentence in Paragraph 6.
   After nearly 200 years of campaigning, the position of women in society in most countries has improved greatly, but many women still face <u>incredible</u> difficulties.
   a. ☐ impressive　　b. ☐ many　　c. ☐ unbelievable　　d. ☐ unnecessary

2. When did feminism start?
   b. ☐ the mid-19th century　　b. ☐ 1975　　c. ☐ 2012
   d. ☐ 2016

3. In which country do women need a letter written by their father or husband before they can get a job?
   a. ☐ Ethiopia　　　　　　　　　b. ☐ Saudi Arabia
   c. ☐ Ghana　　　　　　　　　　d. ☐ Bangladesh

4. On average, women live _____ years longer than men.

    a. ☐ 2   **b.** ☐ 3   **c.** ☐ 5   **d.** ☐ 15

Summary

① 32

Fill each space with the best word or phrase from the list below.

submissive   organized   (give) birth to   prevented   property   citizens

The men who 1) _____ the first cities and towns decided that women should be their 2) _____. Even today, many thousands of years later, society still often expects women to be modest and 3) _____. This has 4) _____ many women from studying, researching, working, and taking part in government in the same way as men. We can never have a truly fair and just society if we treat the mothers that 5) _____ us as second-class 6) _____. Our future path is clear. Men and women must work together to create a better future — as equal partners.

What do YOU think?

Choose ONE of the statements below. Do you agree or disagree with it? Why? Prepare a short response giving your opinion.

> ▶ The next prime minister of Japan should be a woman.
> ▶ Achieving gender equality is not important.

....

....

....

....

> *A woman's place is like a man's place. It is where her work is, wherever she can do the most good; wherever she serves herself best without invading anyone else.*
>
> Gertrude Breslau Hunt (1869-1952)
> American author

Chapter 5: The Internet of Things

This Changes Everything

Useful Words

Choose a word or phrase from the list below to complete each sentence.

1. The _____ on your heater helps to maintain a certain temperature in a room.

2. Many people doing exercise wear a device to _____ their heart rate.

3. With more and more cars on the road, _____ in many major cities is getting slower.

4. In Greek mythology, Pandora's Box is said to have _____ all the troubles of the world.

5. Many companies publish _____ reports detailing their business results for the year.

| contained | monitor | annual | traffic flow | thermostat |

Reading

① 33~39

33

1 Imagine living in a world where you are woken by your favorite music in the morning, where your bathroom checks your health, where your refrigerator automatically orders fresh food, where your car starts automatically, then drives you to work while you read a book or surf the Internet, and where your morning coffee is ready at your desk when you arrive. This kind of connected and automated world may soon be possible with the Internet of Things.

34

2 The Internet of Things is possible because of the incredible power of modern computers. The first computers, such as the Harwell CADET built in England in

1955, contained around 200 transistors. By contrast, just one of the microchips in a modern computer or smartphone contains around 20 billion transistors. As a result, computer speeds have increased from 125 kHz in 1955 to 5 GHz in 2018. In other words, computers in 2018 are 40,000 times faster than computers in 1955. Similarly, wireless connection speeds have increased from 2 Mbps in 1997 to up to 20 Gbps for the newest 5G networks in 2018. That means that 5G networks can transfer data 10,000 times faster than the original 1G networks. The combination of cheap, powerful computer chips, ubiquitous wireless communication, and the Internet means that almost anything can be connected to the Internet, hence the name, the Internet of Things. But what can the Internet of Things actually do to make our lives better?

3 One use of the Internet of Things is to create a smart home. This means that the doors, security, heating, and electrical appliances are all connected to the owner's smartphone via the Internet. As a result, the owner can use their smartphone as a house key, and monitor and control their home using a smartphone app. Some of this technology is already available. For example, Nest Labs in the United States has sold smart thermostats since 2011. These thermostats learn the owner's schedules and preferred temperatures, and then plan the heating and cooling of rooms in the way that uses the least energy. The Dutch company Philips has developed a smart lighting system called Philips Hue, which allows people to use a smartphone to adjust the color and the intensity of the lighting in their room to match how they feel. In the kitchen, an appliance such as the LG Internet refrigerator allows family members to share messages, order food, download recipes, and watch TV. The refrigerator also monitors and provides information about the temperature and the freshness of the food inside it.

In the era of the Internet of Things, it will be possible to use applications to control all kinds of appliances. In this case, a coffee-lover makes a cup of coffee using a smartphone.

4 Cities can also benefit enormously from the Internet of Things. By collecting data from smartphones, cars, and sensors around the city, it is possible to measure traffic flow, the movement of people, parking availability, pollution levels, and energy use. Machines, bridges, and buildings will contain sensors that will alert engineers when they need maintenance. This data will allow city planners to save energy and make our cities cleaner, safer, more convenient, and more pleasant places to live in. As self-driving cars become more common, the collecting and sharing of traffic data could even mean that traffic jams become a thing of the past.

5 The Internet of Things also allows us to monitor ourselves. Many people already use devices such as Fitbit to monitor and record their activity data. Combining this data with data from other smart devices, such as that collected by the smart toilets being developed by the Japanese company Symax, will allow people to get a much better idea of their levels of health and fitness. The data could even be sent directly to doctors, and put an end to the annual health check.

In the era of the Internet of Things, entire cities will be connected to a network of sensors and devices.

6 The Internet of Things clearly offers us a lot of potential benefits. However, the Internet of Things also raises multiple difficult questions about security, privacy, freedom of choice, and anonymity. Is privacy possible in a world where everybody — and everything — is watching you? Furthermore, who should have access to the data collected about you? Your family? The government? The police? Your boss? And what about security? There are many examples of technology companies and governments making foolish mistakes with people's data. For example, in 2017, it was discovered that CloudPets, Internet-connected stuffed toys, could be hacked to record what the children playing with them were doing. It was also discovered that U.S. manufacturer Spiral Toys was storing data about its users in its own database. In February 2017, hackers stole the data of 800,000 customers from the company.

7 The Internet of Things has arrived, and it could change our world as much as smartphones and the Internet did before it. Once everything is connected, we will benefit from greater efficiency, convenience, safety, and health-monitoring. However, once everything is connected, we might possibly lose all of our privacy. Once everything is connected, it may be possible for criminals to hack everything. The future will be amazing, but perhaps also a little scary, and it is up to us to make sure that the Internet of Things leads to a utopia and not a dystopia.

NOTES

the Internet of Things (= IoT)「モノのインターネット」身の回りのあらゆるモノがインターネットにつながること。コンピューターやスマートフォンといった情報・通信機器だけでなく、あらゆる物体・製品（モノ）に通信機能を持たせ、インターネット接続や個々の「モノ」の相互通信により、さまざまな機能を実現する。　**transistor**「トランジスタ」電気の流れをコントロールする部品。ゲルマニウム、ケイ素などを利用して増幅・発振・スイッチングの作用をする半導体素子の総称。
by contrast「一方，それに反して」　**kHz** (= kilohertz)「キロヘルツ」周波数の単位　**GHz** (= gigahertz)「ギガヘルツ」周波数の単位。10 の 9 乗ヘルツ。　**bps** (= bits per second)「ビーピーエス」データ伝送速度、つまり通信速度の基本単位。1 秒間に伝送されるビット数。英数字 1 文字は 8 ビット、日本語 1 文字は 16 ビットで送信。　**Mbps** ※ Chapter 3 を参照　**Gbps** (= gigabits per second)「ギガビット／秒；ギガビット毎秒」Mbps の 1,000 倍に当たる。　**5G** (= 5th generation)「第 5 世代移動通信システム」現在規格の検討が進められている次世代通信システム。2020 年代に想定される IoT（モノのインターネット）化に対応した超高速・超大容量のネットワーク。日本では東京五輪開催の 2020 年 7 月までの商用化が目指されている。　**ubiquitous**「至る所にある」　**app** (= application)「アプリケーション」通称はアプリ。　**Nest Labs**「ネストラボ」米国の企業（2010 年〜）。Apple の iPod の発案者として知られるトニー・ファデル氏が創業者。2011 年に人工知能搭載型のサーモスタット（温度調節装置）Nest Learning Thermostat を発売し大ヒット商品となった。
Phillips「フィリップス」オランダを本拠地とする総合電機機器メーカー。家電製品、医療機器、ヘルスケア製品、照明まで幅広く事業を展開している。1891 年創業。　**LG** (= LG Electronics Inc.)「LG エレクトロニクス」韓国ソウル市に本社を置く総合電子機器メーカー。1958 年に GoldStar として設立。　**intensity**「強度，（色の）彩度」　**city planner**「都市設計家」　**traffic jam**「交通渋滞」　**Fitbit**「フィットビット」腕に巻くなど、身に着けるだけで日々の健康状態を記録し、そのデータをインターネット上で管理するなどできるスマートデバイス。米国のフィットビット社の製品。
Symax「サイマックス」ヘルスケア IoT デバイスを使ったサービスやプラットフォーム（機構）を開発する企業。2014 年設立。　**anonymity**「匿名性」　**access** (n)「近づく（入手する・利用する）権利」　**stuffed toy**「ぬいぐるみ」　**hack**「ハッカー行為（コンピューターシステムに不正侵入する）を行う；ハッキングする」　**lead**「通じる，つながる」All roads lead to Rome.（ことわざ）
utopia「ユートピア，理想郷」　**dystopia**「ディストピア，暗黒郷，反ユートピア」

Chapter 5   **The Internet of Things** – *This Changes Everything*

Questions for Understanding

Part 1 *Look at the following statements. Write T if the statement is true, and F if it is false. Write the number of the paragraph where you find the answer in the parenthesis.*

1. Many people dream about a world where your refrigerator automatically orders your food.

   T/F
   (#   )

2. The Internet of Things can be used to make a smart home.

   T/F
   (#   )

3. The Internet of Things may be able to eliminate traffic accidents.

   T/F
   (#   )

4. To connect to the Internet of Things, we may have to give up our privacy.

   T/F
   (#   )

Part 2 *Look at the questions below. Check the best answer for each.*

1. How much faster are 5G networks than 1G networks?
   a. ☐ About 20 Gbps   b. ☐ About 10,000 times
   c. ☐ About 125 kHz   d. ☐ About 40,000 times

2. Choose the phrase that has the closest meaning to "it is up to us to" in the following sentence in Paragraph 7.
   The future will be amazing, but perhaps also a little scary, and <u>it is up to us to</u> make sure that the Internet of Things leads to a utopia and not a dystopia.
   a. ☐ we must   b. ☐ we will   c. ☐ we may   d. ☐ we can

3. With the Internet of Things, what might it be easier to find in a city?
   a. ☐ an Internet connection   b. ☐ city planners
   c. ☐ a parking space   d. ☐ bridges

4. What did criminals hack in 2017?
   a. ☐ pollution sensors   b. ☐ smart toilets
   c. ☐ self-driving cars   d. ☐ stuffed toys

27

Summary

Fill each space with the best word from the list below.

| adjust | incredible | anonymity | devices | potential | appliances |

The future world made possible by the Internet of Things sounds 1) _____. It will be a world where large numbers of sensors and electronic 2) _____ will be able to connect and communicate with each other via the Internet. We will also be able to monitor our lives from 3) _____, such as smartphones. While the 4) _____ for this technology is tremendous, there are also many concerns. Privacy and security are two of the main issues, and it will be increasingly hard to protect our 5) _____. Everyone will clearly have to 6) _____ to the various opportunities and challenges this new technology brings.

What do YOU think?

Choose ONE of the statements below. Do you agree or disagree with it? Why? Prepare a short response giving your opinion.

▶ Despite some concerns, the Internet of Things will bring great benefits to society.
▶ The Internet of Things will just be a way to give more control to the government and increase criminal activity.

....
....
....
....

> *As the Internet of Things advances, the very notion of a clear dividing line between reality and virtual reality becomes blurred, sometimes in creative ways.*
>
> Geoff Mulgan (1961-)
> CEO of Nesta

Chapter 6
The Supercomputer in Your Pocket
How Cell Phones Are Changing the World

Useful Words

Choose a word or phrase from the list below to complete each sentence.

1. NASA and JAXA are the U.S. and Japanese space _____.
2. I have 86 billion _____ in my brain. A cockroach only has 1 million. So why can't I catch it?
3. After she graduated, she became a _____ at Toyota.
4. I'm so angry! A _____ touched me while I was on the train!
5. I couldn't _____ any money from the ATM because I forgot my PIN.

| molester | staff member | neurons | agencies | withdraw |

Reading

① 41~46

41

1 The first computer to be called a supercomputer was the CDC 6600. From 1964 until 1969, it was the world's fastest and most powerful computer. The CDC 6600 operated at a speed of 10 MHz, had a memory of 64 KB, and it had a performance of 3 megaFLOPS. Fifty years later in 2014, Apple Inc. released the iPhone 6. The iPhone 6 operated at a speed of 1.4 GHz, had a memory of 1 GB, and it had a performance of 76.8 gigaFLOPS. Compared to the CDC 6600, the iPhone 6 was 140 times faster, had a memory that

5

10

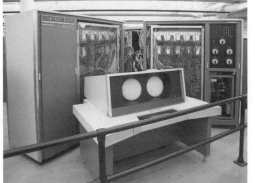

The CDC 6600 — the first supercomputer

was 15,625 times larger, and its performance was 25,600 times greater. Furthermore, while just over 100 CDC 6600 computers were sold to national laboratories such as the Los Alamos National Laboratory in the United States, and international research agencies like CERN in Europe, more than 200 million ordinary people bought an
5 iPhone 6.

42 🎧
CD

2 The incredible computing power of our smartphones is what allows us to use them to play games, watch videos, take pictures, and surf the Internet, as well as (occasionally) make phone calls. However, while for many of us the main benefits of a smartphone are that we are never bored and can be contacted anywhere at any
10 time, smartphones are also changing the world in other, less obvious, ways.

43 🎧
CD

3 *Money*: Using our smartphones as electronic wallets can be a very convenient and easy way to pay for things when we are shopping or traveling. On some days, we may not use any cash at all, and the number of cash transactions in some countries is decreasing every year. For example, 40 percent of all consumer transactions used cash
15 in the United States in 2012, but only 32 percent were in cash in 2015. In fact, some U.S. banks have created smartphone apps that replace the cards traditionally used to withdraw money from ATMs. However, using electronic wallets on our phones instead of cash can have huge benefits in poorer countries. M-Pesa (pesa means "money" in Swahili) is a money transfer app for mobile phones. It began in 2007
20 and was first used in Kenya and Tanzania in East Africa. By 2016, M-Pesa had nearly 30 million users in 10 countries, including Afghanistan, Egypt, India, Romania, and Albania, who made nearly 6 billion transactions. M-Pesa allows its users to transfer money via a text message secured by a PIN (Personal Identification Number). It has been so successful because it reduces crime and corruption. When the Afghan
25 government used M-Pesa to pay its police officers in 2008, it quickly discovered that 10 percent of its employees did not exist — criminals had created fake staff members so that they could steal their pay.

44 🎧
CD

4 *Health*: It is common today to use our smartphones to monitor our health. There are apps that help us to track our activity level, the calories we eat, our heart rate,
30 and even how well we sleep. But our smartphones can be used for more sophisticated health monitoring as well. In 2017, Microsoft developed a smartphone app called GazeSpeak. This app uses a smartphone's camera to allow people to communicate just by moving their eyes. This will help people who are paralyzed, such as sufferers of motor neuron disease. In 2013, two groups of scientists, one at the Technical

30

University of Denmark, and one at Kwansei Gakuin University in Japan, developed systems that allow smartphones to measure a person's brain activity. These systems could be useful in poor countries that cannot afford the expensive systems used in rich countries.

5 *Security*: Smartphones can also help to keep us safe. On April 15, 2013, terrorists attacked the annual marathon race in the U.S. city of Boston. To help identify the terrorists, the police asked people to send photos and videos of the event to them. Thousands did, and the terrorists were quickly identified and found. In 2014, a 20-year-old Japanese woman was attacked by a molester. Fortunately, he was quickly arrested because the woman used her smartphone to take a picture of her attacker. Japanese police made it even easier for people to report crimes in 2016, when they released the Digi Police app for smartphones. The app also features an alarm that women can use if they are attacked by a molester. But what if the police are the criminals? In 2016 in Ivory Coast in West Africa, a police officer shot an unarmed man in the back as he ran away. Then the police officer shot the man in the head, killing him. We know this because an onlooker recorded the scene using his smartphone. While the vast majority of police officers are good people, there will always be some who abuse the power they have. Today, smartphones make it easy to identify such criminals, and make it very difficult for them to hide their crimes.

Smartphones are changing the world for everybody

6 Smartphones are an incredibly useful technology. Although they have some drawbacks, used well, smartphones can keep us entertained, in touch, healthy, and safe. Step by step, smartphones are changing the world, by giving us the tools we need to make it a better place.

NOTES

MHz (= megahertz)「メガヘルツ」**GHz** (= gigahertz)「ギガヘルツ」共に周波数の単位。 **KB** (= kilobyte)「キロバイト」**GB** (= gigabyte)「ギガバイト」共にコンピューターの情報量の単位。1キロバイトは1024バイト。1ギガバイトは1024メガバイト（MB）。 **FLOPS**「フロップス」コンピューターの演算性能を示す指標の1つ。 **Los Alamos National Laboratory**「ロスアラモス国立研究所」米ニューメキシコ州に第2次世界大戦中、原子爆弾の開発を目的とする「マン

ハッタン計画」のために設立された国立研究機関。広島、長崎に投下された原爆を製造した施設。
CERN (= European Organization for Nuclear Research)「欧州共同原子核研究所」ジュネーブにある素粒子物理学の研究機関。欧州を中心とする 21 カ国で共同運営する。1952 年に発足した際の名称が Conseil Européen pour la Recherche Nucléaire で、その略称 CERN が現在も使われている。
transaction「(一回のひとまとまりの) 処理」　**ATM** (= automatic teller machine)「現金自動預払機」　**Swahili**「スワヒリ語」東アフリカで広く使用されている言語で、ケニアとタンザニアの公用語。　**Romania**「ルーマニア」**Albania**「アルバニア」共に東欧の国。　**text message** 携帯電話のショートメッセージ　**PIN** (= Personal Identification Number)「暗証番号，個人識別番号」
corruption「不正行為」　**Digi Police** 日本の警視庁公認の無料アプリ。犯罪発生情報や最寄りの警察署を地図上で表示する「警視庁 MAP」、警視庁犯罪抑止対策本部によるツイッター表示、防犯ブザーなどの機能がある。　**Ivory Coast** コートジボワール (Côte d'Ivoire) 共和国の英語名
abuse「乱用する」　**drawback**「欠点」

Questions for Understanding

Part 1　*Look at the following statements. Write T if the statement is true, and F if it is false. Write the number of the paragraph where you find the answer in the parenthesis.*

1. Modern research agencies use iPhones instead of traditional supercomputers.

   T/F
   (#　　　)

2. The passage implies that smartphones may replace cash in the future.

   T/F
   (#　　　)

3. Only smartphone users in wealthy countries will benefit from new health apps.

   T/F
   (#　　　)

4. According to the passage, smartphones can help to protect us from criminals.

   T/F
   (#　　　)

Part 2　*Look at the questions below. Check the best answer for each.*

1. Compared to the CDC 6600, how many times larger was the memory of the iPhone 6?

   a. ☐ 76.8　　　b. ☐ 140　　　c. ☐ 15,625　　　d. ☐ 200 million

2. Choose the word that has the closest meaning to "sophisticated" in the following sentence in Paragraph 4.

   But our smartphones can be used for more <u>sophisticated</u> health monitoring as well.

   a. ☐ attractive　　b. ☐ expensive　　c. ☐ complex　　d. ☐ useful

3. How do people using GazeSpeak communicate?

   a. ☐ With their ears　　　　　b. ☐ With their eyes
   c. ☐ With text messages　　　d. ☐ With their brain activity

Chapter 6 **The Supercomputer in Your Pocket** – *How Cell Phones Are Changing the World*

4. How did a Japanese woman catch a molester?
   a. ☐ By taking a picture of him   b. ☐ By taking a video of him
   c. ☐ By sending him a message   d. ☐ By attacking him

Summary

① 47

Fill each space with the best word or phrase from the list below.

supercomputers	onlookers	at any time	monitor
sophisticated	transactions		

Perhaps because we use them every day, it is easy to forget how powerful the computers in our smartphones are. Now, researchers are taking advantage of that power to develop 1) _____ new apps that go far beyond simple messaging and games. Apps that allow us to shop may signal the end of cash 2) _____. Others let us 3) _____ our health 4) _____. Still others allow us to stop being 5) _____ and actively protect ourselves and others from crime. These pocket 6) _____ will become ever more important in our daily lives.

What do YOU think?

Choose ONE of the statements below. Do you agree or disagree with it? Why? Prepare a short response giving your opinion.

▶ Using smartphones to buy things is convenient, so we should stop using cash.
▶ The world would be a better place if everybody had a smartphone.

....

....

....

....

Every once in a while a revolutionary product comes along that changes everything.

Steve Jobs (1955-2011)
Co-founder of Apple Inc.

33

Chapter 7

Land, Sea, and Air

How Drones Are Changing Our Lives

Useful Words

Choose a word from the list below to complete each sentence.

1. The criminal was caught after a shopper _____ him in a local shop.
2. If you don't get enough sleep, it can _____ your health.
3. The customs officials at the airport decided to _____ his suitcase.
4. You can use certain applications to record and _____ your bodyweight.
5. The child accidentally disturbed a bee's nest and was chased by a _____ of bees.

| inspect | spotted | swarm | track | affect |

Reading

① 48~55

48

1 Have you ever seen a drone? Many people think that drones, also known as unmanned aerial vehicles (UAV), are a recent invention. However, UAVs have existed since Austria attacked the Italian city of Venice in 1849 using hot air balloons. Why do we call UAVs drones? Beginning in the 1920s, the British Royal Navy started
5 building remote-controlled UAVs that battleships could use for target practice. Two of these UAVs were called the Queen Bee and the Queen Wasp. In 1935, when the U.S. Navy developed its own UAVs, it named them after male bees — drones.

49

2 Until the 1960s, UAVs were mostly used by the military for target practice. However, during the 1960s, the United States began using UAVs to spy on China and
10 Vietnam. One reason for this is that spy planes were very expensive, but could easily

be shot down by missiles. While the UAVs were also expensive, there was no danger of a pilot being killed or captured. By the 1990s, improvements in technology meant that drones could also carry weapons. These new combat drones were first used by the U.S. during the 1991 Gulf War. By 2015, more than 6,000 people around the world had been killed by U.S. drone attacks, and more than 50 countries had built their own combat drones.

3 Fortunately, drones can also be used to save lives. In Australia in early 2018, a drone was used to help rescue two swimmers that were in trouble off the coast of New South Wales. During a training exercise aimed to limit shark attacks, it spotted that the swimmers were in trouble and dropped a flotation device. Firefighters in the U.S. are using drones to provide information about fires and to search for missing people. Drones were also used for mapping areas affected by the 2015 earthquake in Nepal. In Japan, drones were used to inspect the Fukushima Daiichi nuclear power plant after the March 11, 2011 earthquake and tsunami.

4 The police have also found ways to use drones. For example, police in the French region of Bordeaux use drones to spot speeding drivers. In Britain, the police are using drones to track suspects and monitor crime situations. In the U.S., law enforcement officers have used surveillance drones to monitor traffic, to patrol national borders, and to catch drug smugglers. While the police can use helicopters for the same tasks, drones are much cheaper, quieter, and smaller than helicopters. As a result, it is much harder for criminals to realize they are being tracked.

5 Drones also have a wide range of commercial and industrial applications. Water and energy companies use drones to inspect pipelines, while mining companies use them to explore remote areas, and farmers use them to spray and inspect crops. For example, PrecisionHawk's Lancaster drone can monitor the weather and temperature, and check crops on the ground for disease. Companies like Amazon and United Parcel Service (UPS) may soon start to use drones to deliver their products. In fact, the first drone-delivered products were Domino's pizzas delivered in New Zealand in 2016.

This may one day be a common sight in our skies: a drone delivering a package.

6 Today, almost anybody can buy a drone. With drones costing as little as $40, it is no surprise that by 2018 more than 1.5 million had been sold in the U.S. alone. This easy availability of drones has meant that scientists can use them to study birds, animals, and nature in completely new ways. It has also encouraged drone hobbyists to test their flying skills against each other. Drone racing began in Australia in 2014. By 2018, the largest drone racing organization, the Drone Racing League, had professional drone racers competing in events that were broadcast to 75 countries.

7 However, that fact that anybody can buy a drone means that they can be used badly or foolishly as well. In 2017, U.S. police caught a man using a drone to fly 6 kilograms of drugs from Mexico into the U.S. In 2017, a drone hit an aircraft as it was landing in Quebec, Canada. Although the plane's wing was damaged, it was able to land safely. In Australia in 2015, and in Canada in 2016, athletes competing in races were hit and injured by drones that were filming the races. In South Africa in 2016, a drone smashed through a window and hit an office worker in the head. In Japan in 2015, a man flew a drone containing radioactive sand from Fukushima Prefecture onto the prime minister's official residence. In 2018, terrorists used a swarm of 10 home-made drones armed with bombs to attack a Russian military base in Syria. As a result of incidents like these, many countries have passed laws limiting how high, how fast, where, and when people can fly drones, and the police have developed their own "anti-drone" drones.

Drones have also been used widely by the military for unmanned surveillance and attacking remote locations.

8 Drones can be used in many ways, both good and bad. It may not be long until drones deliver your online shopping and your take-out food. However, it is important to ensure that drones are used safely and in ways that will help improve our lives.

Chapter 7   **Land, Sea, and Air** — *How Drones Are Changing Our Lives*

NOTES

unmanned aerial vehicle (UAV)「無人航空機」　**Venice**「ベニス」イタリア語名はVenezia(ベネチア)　**target practice**「射撃訓練」　**wasp**「カリバチ（狩蜂）」　**drone**「ドローン（無人飛行機），雄バチ」　**the 1991 Gulf War**「1991年の湾岸戦争」1990年8月のイラクによるクウェート侵攻をきっかけとした国際紛争。国連の決議によって編成された米国を中心とする多国籍軍が1991年1月にイラクへの攻撃を開始、2月末までにはクウェートを解放した。　**New South Wales**「ニューサウスウェールズ州」オーストラリア南東部の州で、同国最大の都市シドニーと同国の首都キャンベラがある。　**map**「地図を描く」　**the 2015 earthquake in Nepal** 2015年4月にネパールで起きたマグニチュード（M）7.8の地震。首都カトマンズを含む広い地域で甚大な被害が発生し、周辺国を含めた死者数は9,000人を超えた。　**law enforcement officer**「法執行官」警察官、検察官、捜査官など。　**surveillance drone**「無人偵察機」　**smuggler**「密輸業者」　**mining company**「鉱業会社」　**crop**「農作物」　**PrecisionHawk** ドローンを活用した効率的なデータ収集・解析サービスを提供する米国の企業　**United Parcel Service (UPS)**「ユナイテッド・パーセル・サービス(UPS)」1907年に設立された米国の貨物配送および宅配便サービスの会社。**radioactive**「放射能のある」

Questions for Understanding

Part 1 *Look at the following statements. Write T if the statement is true, and F if it is false. Write the number of the paragraph where you find the answer in the parenthesis.*

1. Unmanned aerial vehicles first appeared in the 20th century.

    T/F ☐

    (#   )

2. Unmanned aerial vehicles have been carrying weapons since the 1960s.

    T/F ☐

    (#   )

3. Drones have been used to track criminals and patrol borders.

    T/F ☐

    (#   )

4. Drones are also used by criminals to smuggle drugs.

    T/F ☐

    (#   )

Part 2 *Look at the questions below. Check the best answer for each.*

1. Which of the following is a key benefit of drones for the military?
   a. ☐ They are hard for the enemy to detect.
   b. ☐ They are much cheaper than manned planes.
   c. ☐ They avoid using actual human pilots.
   d. ☐ They are better at shooting weapons than humans.

37

2. According to the passage, what can drones not do?
   - a. ☐ Rescue people
   - b. ☐ Give information about fires
   - c. ☐ Capture criminals
   - d. ☐ Identify speeding drivers

3. According to the passage, what can the PrecisionHawk's Lancaster drone do?
   - a. ☐ Monitor the weather
   - b. ☐ Deliver pizza
   - c. ☐ Deliver products for companies like UPS and Amazon.
   - d. ☐ Inspect pipelines

4. How was the Japanese prime minister affected by a drone?
   - a. ☐ A swarm of drones attacked him with bombs.
   - b. ☐ A drone tried to crash into his plane.
   - c. ☐ A drone tried to crash directly into him.
   - d. ☐ A drone carried a harmful substance close to him.

Summary

① 56

Fill each space with the best word from the list below.

| surveillance   availability   hobbyists   smugglers   aiming   unmanned |

1) _____ aerial vehicles have been with us for over 160 years but they have developed dramatically over that time. They are now used for a host of different purposes from aerial 2) _____ to saving lives. They are also used by 3) _____ who enjoy racing them. It is not surprising that they can be used for both good and bad. For example, drug 4) _____ and terrorists have made use of drones. The wide 5) _____ of drones will increasingly make them commonplace in our lives. Governments around the world are 6) _____ to regulate the use of drones to improve safety and ensure that they benefit us rather than do harm.

Chapter 7   **Land, Sea, and Air** – *How Drones Are Changing Our Lives*

What do YOU think?

Choose ONE of the statements below. Do you agree or disagree with it? Why? Prepare a short response giving your opinion.

> ▶ A world with a lot more drones will be a better place.
>
> ▶ Drones should be limited to military use only.

....

....

....

....

> *Drones overall will be more impactful than I think people recognize, in positive ways to help society.*
>
> Bill Gates (1955-)
> Co-founder of Microsoft

Chapter 8 Forever Young

The Quest for Eternal Youth

Useful Words

Choose a word or phrase from the list below to complete each sentence.

1. When we read the _____ of Plato and Confucius, we can learn about how to live our lives well.

2. I love _____ stories where the heroes change the world, like the *Harry Potter* series or *Journey to the West*.

3. According to the World Bank, the _____ of Japanese people rose from 67.7 years in 1960 to 83.7 years in 2015.

4. Smoking for years can _____ health problems like cancer, heart disease, and blindness.

5. The Dutch are the tallest people in the world. The _____ heights for men and women are 1.81 meters and 1.69 meters respectively.

| epic | life expectancy | average | philosophy | result in |

Reading

① 57~63

57

1 The famous idiom, that it "is impossible to be sure of anything but death and taxes," was first written by Christopher Bullock, English dramatist, in 1716. However, people have been trying to avoid both of these things throughout history, and the idea of living forever has been an important part of many cultures. The
5 oldest known story, the *Epic of Gilgamesh*, was first written down 4,000 years ago in Sumer. It is about a king who seeks eternal life. In 210 BCE, Qin Shi Huangdi, the first emperor of China, wanted to rule China forever. So he sent the magician Xu Fu to find the elixir of life. Xu Fu left China with a fleet of 60 ships, but he did not

return. Some legends say that he traveled to Japan. Life after death — at least for believers — is the promise of many religions, including Christianity, Hinduism, and Islam. But is immortality really possible? And if it was, would we really want to live forever?

2 According to the World Health Organization, in 2015, the country with the longest-lived people was Japan. Japanese men have an average life expectancy of 80.5 years, and Japanese women have an average life expectancy of 86.8 years. These are averages, and some people live a lot longer. The world's oldest man, Jiroemon Kimura, was 116 years old when he died, and the oldest woman, Jeanne Calment, lived for 122 years. Yet these long lives are as nothing compared to some plants and animals. Some sharks and koi fish can live for 200 years. The Ocean quahog clam can live for more than 500 years. The American Great Basin Bristlecone pine tree can live for over 4,000 years. Some small jellyfish, known as medusas, may even be immortal. These jellyfish can change from a baby to an adult, and then back into a baby again. So is it possible for us to live longer lives too?

Some trees, like this Great Basin Bristlecone Pine, can live for thousands of years.

3 The answer to that question is … maybe. Scientists have discovered that severely limiting how much food animals can eat can result in their living longer lives. However, while this may result in mice living up to 50 percent longer, monkeys only gain a few extra years. Nonetheless, some people have tried it for themselves by limiting how much they eat to between 1,500 and 1,800 calories per day (compared to around 2,000 calories per day recommended by doctors in developed countries). Unfortunately, while they are very healthy, they do not seem to be living longer than average lives.

4 Fictional vampires like Dracula live forever by drinking the blood of their victims. Astonishingly, in 2010, researchers at the Harvard Stem Cell Institute discovered that old mice were rejuvenated, that is they became younger, when their blood was replaced by the blood of young mice. Similar results were found in 2016, when old mice were given blood plasma (the liquid part of blood) from human teenagers. However, transfusing blood from one person to another takes a long time, can result in allergic reactions, and can spread diseases like HIV or hepatitis. Instead, scientists are now trying to discover chemicals in the blood that cause rejuvenation in order to make drugs with the same effects.

5 A more extreme way to achieve immortality is to copy our minds and transfer them into new biological bodies or robots. While a common concept in science fiction, surprisingly, it may be possible one day. In 2013, scientists at the Massachusetts Institute of Technology (MIT) were able to implant simple memories into the brain of a mouse. In 2014, scientists at the University of Washington were able to send a thought from one person's brain across the Internet into a different person's brain. However, these technologies are very new, and computers powerful enough to store a copy of a human brain simply do not exist yet. Furthermore, the concept of copying your mind raises some interesting philosophical questions. Would a copy of you really be you? If there were two copies, would they both be you?

6 But should we really be trying to achieve immortality at all? Any technology that could ensure eternal life would be very expensive. A world where only the rich could live forever may not be a very nice place. In addition, if everybody could live forever, would they still want to have children? How would immortality affect the environment? Furthermore, if you could live forever, what would you do? What if you had to work forever, and never be able to retire?

7 Throughout human history, the desire to live forever and never die has been an important part of human culture. It has driven progress in medicine, technology, and philosophy. Perhaps in the end the greatest benefit of the pursuit of immortality is not that we will ever achieve it, but rather what it teaches us about ourselves.

What does immortality mean to you?

NOTES

the Epic of Gilgamesh『ギルガメシュ叙事詩』メソポタミア神話の英雄ギルガメシュの遍歴を描いている。　**Sumer**「シュメール」西アジアのチグリス川とユーフラテス川の下流域を指した地名で、古代文明の発祥の地。　**Qin Shi Huangdi**「秦（Qin）の始皇帝」　**Xu Fu**「徐福」秦代の方士（ほうし＝特殊な技術を身に付けた人）　**elixir of life**「不老不死の霊薬」　**immortality**「不死」　**World Health Organization**「世界保健機関」国連の専門機関。「全ての人が可能な最高

の健康水準に到達すること」を目的として 1948 年に設立された。　**Kimura Jiroemon**「木村次郎右衛門」(1897-2013)　**Jeanne Calment**「ジャンヌ・カルマン（1875-1997)」フランス人女性で、122 歳と 164 日で亡くなった最も長寿の人。　**Ocean quahog**「ホンビノスガイ」北米大西洋岸原産の二枚貝　**pine tree**「松の木」　**jellyfish**「クラゲ」　**calorie** ここで使用されている 1 calorie（大カロリー）は栄養学で用いられる熱量単位で、1 kilocalorie（小カロリー）に相当する。**vampire**「吸血鬼」　**result in**「〜という結果をもたらす；〜に帰結する」　**Harvard Stem Cell Institute**「ハーバード幹細胞研究所」　**rejuvenate**「若返らせる」　**plasma**「血漿（けっしょう）」　**hepatitis**「肝炎」　**Massachusetts Institute of Technology**「マサチューセッツ工科大学（MIT）」米マサチューセッツ州ケンブリッジにある私立大学。1865 年開校。　**the University of Washington**「ワシントン大学」米ワシントン州シアトルにある州立の総合大学

Questions for Understanding

Part 1　*Look at the following statements. Write T if the statement is true, and F if it is false. Write the number of the paragraph where you find the answer in the parenthesis.*

1. The idea of immortality has appeared in many cultures and religions.

   T/F _____ (# ___)

2. According to the passage, some animals and plants are immortal.

   T/F _____ (# ___)

3. The passage indicates that there may be more than one route to immortality.

   T/F _____ (# ___)

4. It is suggested that achieving immortality could have drawbacks for society.

   T/F _____ (# ___)

Part 2　*Look at the questions below. Check the best answer for each.*

1. How many years can some koi fish live for?
   a. ☐ 122　　　b. ☐ 200　　　c. ☐ 500　　　d. ☐ 4,000

2. What happened to old mice when they were given less food?
   a. ☐ They lived half as long as usual.
   b. ☐ They lived one and half times as long as usual.
   c. ☐ They lived twice as long as usual.
   d. ☐ They lived a few years longer.

3. What happened to old mice when they were given young blood?
   a. ☐ They grew older.　　　　　b. ☐ They had allergic reactions.
   c. ☐ They grew younger.　　　　d. ☐ They developed hepatitis.

4. What did scientists at MIT do?
   a. ☐ They sent a thought across the Internet.
   b. ☐ They gave old mice new blood.
   c. ☐ They transferred a memory between mice.
   d. ☐ They copied a human brain.

Summary

Fill each space with the best word from the list below.

| affect | pursuit | immortality | emperor | nonetheless | average |

The desire to live forever has been an important part of human civilization since history began. However, not even the most powerful 1) _____ ever achieved eternal life. 2) _____, modern technology and medicine have resulted in us living ever longer lives. Today, Japanese people can expect to live to at least 80 years on 3) _____, and every year more and more people reach 100 years old. Furthermore, recent research indicates that even longer lives, and perhaps even a form of 4) _____, may be possible in the future. While the idea of a never-ending life is attractive, we must think carefully about how the 5) _____ of such technologies might 6) _____ society and the environment. We must make sure that such long lives are worth living.

What do YOU think?

Choose ONE of the statements below. Do you agree or disagree with it? Why? Prepare a short response giving your opinion.

▶ We should solve problems of poverty and disease before finding ways to live longer lives.
▶ I want to live forever.

> *We all die. The goal isn't to live forever. The goal is to create something that will.*
>
> Chuck Palahniuk (1962-)
> American author

Chapter 9

Just Forget It!

The Science of Rewriting Memories

Useful Words

Choose a word or phrase from the list below to complete each sentence.

1. Disney's first _____ in Asia opened in Chiba Prefecture in 1983.

2. In order to _____ how he looked, the spy shaved his head and wore glasses.

3. She couldn't believe that she had been chosen to be a _____ on a TV game show.

4. No matter how hard she tried to _____ it, she could not remember her password.

5. Because his bill was so high, he decided to _____ how much he used his phone.

| reduce | participant | theme park | recall | alter |

Reading

1 Do you have a good memory? Our ability to remember information is amazing. For example, in 2006, Akira Haraguchi memorized the number pi. Unlike most people, who perhaps learn the first three or four digits, Haraguchi memorized 100,000. It took him 16 and a half hours to recite them all. Understanding how people can achieve

How good is your memory?

45

such feats of recall helps us to understand how our memories work and also how they can go wrong.

66

2 Many people are surprised to discover that we have more than one kind of memory. Everything we experience first goes into our short-term memory. If we need
5 to think about that information, it is moved into our working memory. Information in our short-term memory is only stored for a few seconds, while information in our working memory lasts for as long as we are actively thinking about it. Only information that passes into our working memory can become a permanent part of our long-term memory. However, we need to sleep in order to make strong long-term
10 memories. Scientists have found that having too little sleep, or waking people when they are dreaming, can reduce how well they remember information and experiences they had during the previous day. Furthermore, how easily we can remember something depends on how well the memory is connected to other information and also on how often we try to remember it.

67

15 **3** Unfortunately, however, our brains do not record information like a camera or a computer. This means that memory errors can be surprisingly easy to make. While this can be inconvenient when we cannot recall someone's name or the answer to a test, it can have dramatic implications in some situations. For example, of the 350 innocent people the Innocence Project in the United States has helped to free
20 from prison, 70 percent had been incorrectly identified by witnesses or the victims of a crime. But how can the victim of a crime identify the wrong person? When we are in a very stressful situation, such as being involved in a crime, our bodies and brains are focused on surviving and escaping rather than thinking. As a result, much of what we experience is never stored in our long-term memories. When we try to
25 remember what happened, our brains fill in any missing information, and we cannot tell which part of the memory is correct and which is not.

68

4 Furthermore, in 1973, U.S. psychologist Elizabeth Loftus discovered that simply by changing how questions were asked, it was possible to change how people remembered an event. Then, in 1995, she showed that it was quite easy to create
30 completely false memories in people's minds. In fact, all she needed to do was give people four short descriptions of events from their childhood and ask them to remember as much detail as they could about each one. However, one of the events was false. A week later, the participants were asked to describe the four events. Not only did 25 percent of the participants report the false event as a real memory,

46

but when told that one of the events was false, 20 percent of the participants identified a real event from their childhood as the fake event. In another famous experiment in 2002, she asked people if they remembered meeting the cartoon character Bugs Bunny at the Disney World theme park in Florida. Sixteen percent of the participants had a clear memory of shaking hands with Bugs Bunny, even though Bugs Bunny is not a Disney character.

Is Bugs Bunny YOUR favorite Disney character?

5   Elizabeth Loftus showed us that rather than being recorded only once, our memories are modified and altered every time we recall them. Does this mean that it is also possible to erase memories? Scientists at New York University in 2000 gave rats a small electric shock after playing a sound. Not surprisingly, the rats soon became afraid of the sound. However, if the rats were given a drug called propranolol, and then played the sound, they lost their fear. In other words, the drug had erased part of their memory. In 2015, scientists at McGill University in Canada treated victims of the 2015 earthquake in Nepal and the 2015 terrorist attacks in Paris with propranolol. After six weeks, nearly 70 percent of the participants had forgotten the fear and terror they experienced during those events. In 2006, scientists at the State University of New York (SUNY) discovered a drug named ZIP could completely erase memories, at least in mice.

6   Should we be learning how to re-write our memories? Nearly 17 percent of people who experience traumatic events such as natural disasters, wars, or violent crimes, suffer from Post-Traumatic Stress Disorder (PTSD). These people find they cannot forget the event, and this can cause many problems for them and their families. Erasing memories of the stressful event would definitely help these people. But what if criminals or governments used this technology to erase the memories of their crimes? Our memories, however imperfect, are a central part of who we are. We must think very carefully before giving anybody the power to change them.

NOTES

Akira Haraguchi「原口證」56 歳で円周率暗唱世界記録への挑戦を決意し、59 歳で 5 万 4,000 桁の暗唱を達成（世界新記録）。その後記録を更新し、2006 年に 10 万桁を達成した。　**pi**「円周率」 **feat**「偉業」 **short-term memory**「短期記憶」 **working memory**「作動記憶，作業記憶」 **long-term memory**「長期記憶」　**Innocence Project**「イノセンス・プロジェクト」米国で始まった冤罪（えんざい）救済活動のプロジェクト。①冤罪救済②政策・法律提言③誤判の要因排除のための公判を通じた改革④釈放後の生活支援の 4 つの柱からなる。　**witness**「目撃者」 **propranolol**「プロプラノロール」　**the 2015 earthquake in Nepal** ※ Chapter 6 を参照 **the 2015 terrorist attacks in Paris** 2015 年 11 月 13 日にパリ市内と近郊の 6 カ所でほぼ同時に起きたテロ攻撃。過激派組織「イスラム国」がフランスによるシリア空爆への報復とする犯行声明を出した。実行犯は自動小銃を乱射、犠牲者は 19 カ国の 130 人に達した。　**State University of New York**「ニューヨーク州立大学（SUNY）」　**Post-Traumatic Stress Disorder**「心的外傷後ストレス障害（PSTD）」人が通常経験する範囲をはるかに超えた苦悩を経験した後に起きる精神障害。憂鬱、焦燥感、罪の意識、恐怖、悪夢など。

Questions for Understanding

Part 1 *Look at the following statements. Write T if the statement is true, and F if it is false. Write the number of the paragraph where you find the answer in the parenthesis.*

1. According to the passage, our memories are usually very reliable.
   T/F
   (#　　　)

2. We learn from the passage that it is very hard to create false memories.
   T/F
   (#　　　)

3. Scientists have discovered a drug that can remove the emotional part of a memory.
   T/F
   (#　　　)

4. Deleting memories may help some people, but this technology could also be misused.
   T/F
   (#　　　)

Part 2 *Look at the questions below. Check the best answer for each.*

1. What did Akira Haraguchi memorize?
   a. ☐ Three or four digits of pi
   b. ☐ Sixteen digits of pi
   c. ☐ Two thousand six digits of pi
   d. ☐ One hundred thousand digits of pi

Chapter 9   **Just Forget It!** – *The Science of Rewriting Memories*

2. Which of the following is the correct order of the memory process?
   a. ☐ short-term memory → false memory → long-term memory
   b. ☐ short-term memory → working memory → long-term memory
   c. ☐ short-term memory → long-term memory → false memory
   d. ☐ short-term memory → long-term memory → working memory

3. What proportion of people misremembered meeting Bugs Bunny at Disney World?
   a. ☐ 16 percent   b. ☐ 17 percent   c. ☐ 20 percent   d. ☐ 25 percent

4. Choose the word or phrase that has the closest meaning to "modified" in the following sentence in Paragraph 5.
   Elizabeth Loftus showed us that rather than being recorded only once, our memories are <u>modified</u> and altered every time we recall them.
   a. ☐ brought back   b. ☐ changed
   c. ☐ fixed   d. ☐ washed out

Summary

① 71

Fill each space with the best word or phrase from the list below.

| identify | depend on | modify | traumatic | definitely | what if |

While some people like Akira Haraguchi are able to correctly recite huge amounts of information from memory, scientific research has found that we cannot always 1) _____ our memories. Scientists have discovered that our brains fill in any missing information when we recall something. While this is not usually a problem, it sometimes means that victims of crimes 2) _____ the wrong person as a criminal. Psychologists have also found that it is very easy to create false memories, and neuroscientists are researching ways to 3) _____ memories. The ability to reduce the negative consequences that some people experience after being involved in a 4) _____ event could be very helpful, but 5) _____ criminals used the same process to hide their crimes? The potential misuse of this new technology is something we must 6) _____ think about carefully.

49

What do YOU think?

Choose ONE of the statements below. Do you agree or disagree with it? Why? Prepare a short response giving your opinion.

▶ Being able to change our memories would be bad for society.
▶ Erasing the memories of criminals would be better than sending them to prison.

When I was younger, I could remember anything, whether it had happened or not.

Mark Twain (1835-1910)
American author

Chapter 10

I Am Who I Am

Sex, Sexuality, and Gender

Useful Words

Choose a word or phrase from the list below to complete each sentence.

1. They _____ each other when they first met, and got married a year later.

2. Gorillas, chimpanzees, bonobos, and humans are all different _____ of ape.

3. Unfortunately, his smartphone would not _____ his new phone case.

4. _____ to his good grades in science, his grades in art were terrible.

5. This is a picture of my _____ friends' wedding; Sara has black hair and her wife Paula has blond hair.

| species | homosexual | (be) attracted to | in contrast | fit into |

Reading

① 72~77

72

1 Our bodies change a lot when we become teenagers and begin puberty, but in the village of Salinas in the Dominican Republic, some children change a lot more: around 1 percent of girls transform into boys. How is such a thing possible?

2 For hundreds of years, an important idea in European and American society, religion, and science, was that there were two sexes, male and female, and two genders, men and women. Anyone that did not fit into these categories was regarded as unnatural and wrong. However, this idea ignored the evidence from history, from the many different cultures around the world and, most importantly, nature itself.

51

In reality, nature is more complicated, mysterious, and elaborate than most people realize.

Fighting for the right to love. Campaigners for equal rights for homosexual and transgender people fly the Rainbow Flag in London in 2009.

3 One of the most complex natural processes is the creation of a baby. It is so complex, in fact, that at least 25 percent of all human pregnancies fail. Whether you are genetically male (i.e. you have an X and a Y chromosome) or genetically female (i.e. you have two X chromosomes), there is no difference in the body of a fetus (a baby before it has been born) for the first six to eight weeks. After this time, male and female fetuses produce different kinds and amounts of hormones which direct the body to develop into a male or a female. However, since humans have about 30,000 genes and trillions of cells in their bodies, it should be no surprise that sometimes babies develop in unexpected ways. For example, it is estimated that nearly 1.5 percent of people are intersex, which means that they have extra X or Y chromosomes, or that their bodies have not responded to hormones in the usual way. This is why some of the girls in Salinas change into boys when they become teenagers: their bodies did not respond to male hormones before they were born, but do when they become teenagers.

4 As well as our physical sex, our sexuality is also fixed before we are born. Our sexual identity relates to the kind of people we are attracted to, something that most people become very aware of when they become teenagers. The majority of people are heterosexual — they are attracted to people of the opposite sex, but around 4 to 8 percent of people are homosexual or bisexual — they are attracted to people of the same sex, or to both sexes equally. However, while our lifetime sexuality is not something we choose, it is not uncommon to experiment and explore our sexuality when young, and up to 10 percent of people report having had a homosexual experience during their lives. Furthermore, homosexuality has been observed in over 1,500 different species of animals. Scientists are still debating what this means, but it is likely that there is an important reason why some of us are homosexual.

5 The children in Salinas feel like girls when they are girls, and feel like boys when they become boys. In contrast, transgender people have a strong feeling that their identity does not match their physical bodies at all. This affects about 0.3 percent of people, and research has found that the brains of transgender people are more similar to the opposite sex than to their own.

Why shouldn't we marry the one we love?

Many transgender people try to change their lives to better fit their identity. This can mean changing how they dress, the name they use, and even having surgery to change their bodies to the opposite biological sex.

6 Transgender people can experience incredible stress and frustration as they try to make other people understand them. Along with sexual minorities like homosexuals, transgender people are much more likely to experience bullying, violence, discrimination in employment, and to commit suicide. Part of the reason for this is that they do not fit into the idea that there are only two genders, which can make some people feel uncomfortable. This can be especially true during our teenage years, when discovering love and being accepted by our friends are so important.

7 In recent years, things have changed in many countries. After many years of campaigning, same-sex marriage is now legal in more than 20 countries, and some countries are revising their sex and relationship education classes so that children will be better informed about the different kinds of sex, sexuality, and gender. After having an identity imposed on us by society for so long, the time has come for us to accept and respect each person as the individual human beings we are. Ultimately, we will only be successful when everyone can say, "I am what I am. I love who I love. I am who I am. Normal."

NOTES

sex「性（別）」生物学的な性差　**sexuality**「性的指向，性自認」　**gender**「ジェンダー」生物学的な性に対して、社会的・文化的構築物としての性という概念。　**puberty**「思春期」　**Dominican Republic**「ドミニカ共和国」カリブ海のイスパニョーラ島の3分の2を占め、西はハイチと接する。　**elaborate**「複雑な，精緻な」　**pregnancy**「妊娠」　**genetically**

「遺伝子（学）上は」　**chromosome**「染色体」　**fetus**「胎児」　**gene**「遺伝子」　**cell**「細胞」
intersex「間性（個体）」雌雄異体の生物で、雌雄の中間の性的特徴を持つ個体またはその性質。
heterosexual「異性愛の；異性愛者」　**homosexual**「同性愛の；同性愛者」　**bisexual**「両
性愛の；両性愛者」　**experiment** (vi)「（新しいこと・方法）を試してみる」　**transgender**
people「トランスジェンダーの人たち」自身の生物学的性と心の性が一致しないことから、生まれ持
った生物学的性と反対の性で生きようとする人たち。　**biological sex**「生物学的性」　**bullying**
「いじめ」　**discrimination**「差別」　**same-sex marriage**「同性婚」　**revise**「見直す，改
訂する」　**sex and relationship education classes**「"性と人間関係"の授業」　**have ...**
imposed on ~「〜に・・・を押し付ける」

Questions for Understanding

Part 1　*Look at the following statements. Write T if the statement is true, and F if it is false.Write the number of the paragraph where you find the answer in the parenthesis.*

1. According to the passage, some boys in the village of Salinas become girls.

   T/F
   (#　　　)

2. As well as humans, many species of animal also have homosexual members.

   T/F
   (#　　　)

3. Although their bodies change, the children from Salinas are not transgender.

   T/F
   (#　　　)

4. In some countries it is now possible for homosexuals to get married.

   T/F
   (#　　　)

Part 2　*Look at the questions below. Check the best answer for each.*

1. Choose the word that has the closest meaning to "direct" in the following sentence in Paragraph 3.
   After this time, male and female fetuses produce different kinds and amounts of hormones which <u>direct</u> the body to develop into a male or a female.
   a. ☐ force　　　b. ☐ regulate　　　c. ☐ train　　　d. ☐ warn

2. When is our sexuality decided?
   a. ☐ Before we are born　　　b. ☐ When we are children
   c. ☐ When we are teenagers　　d. ☐ When we are married

3. If you are heterosexual, this is your …
   a. ☐ gender　　b. ☐ sex　　　c. ☐ sexuality　　d. ☐ chromosome

4. What percentage of people are transgender?
   a. ☐ 0.3　　　b. ☐ 1.5　　　c. ☐ 4　　　d. ☐ 8

54

Chapter 10   **I Am Who I Am** – *Sex, Sexuality, and Gender*

Summary

① 78

Fill each space with the best word or phrase from the list below.

impose	(be) aware of	gender	heterosexual
similar to	transgender		

It is easy to think that the ideas, traditions, and beliefs that we are used to are "normal." However, that would be a mistake, because it means that we might reject anything or anybody that is not 1) _____ ourselves. For example, while most people feel that their biological sex and their 2) _____ fit together, some people are 3) _____ and feel the opposite. Likewise, while most people are 4) _____, we should 5) _____ the fact that some people are homosexual. Part of becoming a global citizen is revising our ideas of what is "normal" to include people different to ourselves, and learning not to 6) _____ our opinions on others.

What do YOU think?

Choose ONE of the statements below. Do you agree or disagree with it? Why? Prepare a short response giving your opinion.

▶ Marriage should only be between a man and a woman.
▶ School uniforms should be the same for all genders.

....
....
....
....

> *The most authentic thing about us is our capacity to create, to overcome, to endure, to transform, to love, and to be greater than our suffering.*
>
> Ben Okri (1959-)
> Nigerian author

55

Chapter 11

Uber, Airbnb, and TaskRabbit

Collaborative Consumption and the Sharing Economy

Useful Words

Choose a word from the list below to complete each sentence.

1. At five years old, he is already a great skier. He has the _____ to go to the Olympics.

2. The sales manager provided a _____ that the company would double its sales this year.

3. I have decided to _____ an ambitious project: to sail around the world single-handed.

4. Madison Square Garden is a famous _____ for music and sporting events in New York.

5. After the earthquake, the city needed _____ repairs.

| venue | extensive | potential | undertake | guarantee |

Reading

② 02~08

02

1 People have always shared their possessions and time, particularly with their friends and local communities. In the modern era, this sharing of resources has expanded through the use of technology and is called collaborative consumption or the sharing economy. According to Bank of America, the global sharing economy
5 was worth around $250 billion in 2017 and has the potential to be worth $2 trillion by 2025. But what is the sharing economy? It is the use of the Internet, social media, and smartphone apps to connect customers with service providers. For customers, these are convenient and easy to use, while the service providers can earn more money and have control over when, and how often, they work. One well-known example of

56

the sharing economy is carsharing, when people rent a vehicle for a short period of time. This is different from carpooling, which is when a person with a car gives their co-workers a ride to work. What other kinds of services can be found in the sharing economy?

2 Airbnb was founded in 2008, with a simple aim: to help people rent out their empty rooms or houses to visiting guests. In other words, Airbnb lets people turn their homes into hotels, if only for a few days. It has been incredibly successful. Airbnb now operates in 191 countries, has over 4 million listings, and has welcomed more than 200 million people to its properties since its founding. As a customer, you can stay in apartments, villas, yurts, boats, castles, tree houses, and even igloos. Today, similar businesses offer people the ability to rent cars, bicycles, and even pets.

It is amazing where you can stay. A couple win a stay at Dracula's castle in Bran, Romania, as part of a competition sponsored by Airbnb.

3 Since 2009, Uber has been transforming the transportation industry, and today it is reported to have over 1 billion accounts. Anyone with a car (or boat, helicopter, or even auto-rickshaw) can create their own taxi business. Drivers and potential customers create an Uber account, and then the technology matches the two parties. The application also handles payment and provides a review system which helps to establish and maintain trust between the suppliers and customers. Uber was reported to be worth around $50 billion in late 2017.

4 TaskRabbit allows you to rent out your skills and time. On the site you can find someone to help you with a variety of tasks such as helping you fix something or move to a new house. It works very simply. You log into the site and describe the task you would like done. The site then matches you with potential workers and you can talk about the details such as price and schedule. The person will then arrive and do the task. Once it is finished and everyone is happy, the payment is made and the customer leaves a review. TaskRabbit also has a happiness guarantee — it checks all its workers and provides $1 million of insurance for each job undertaken, just in case something goes wrong. The furniture chain Ikea bought TaskRabbit in 2017 for $6.5 billion.

5 Cities are also participating in the sharing economy. In preparation for being a venue during the 2019 Rugby World Cup, Kamaishi City in Iwate Prefecture decided to use the sharing economy to promote itself as a tourist destination. The city predicted that there could be problems with transportation and accommodations during the event, so in October 2016, the city signed a contract with Airbnb to create programs to use farmhouses and other locations in the community. It also developed a bicycle share service called CogiCogi and a car sharing service called ShareNori to offer transportation to visitors during the event.

6 While the sharing economy clearly has many benefits, it has also created disruption and caused problems. Established operators such as hotels and licensed taxi drivers argue that these new businesses can avoid obtaining the permits and extensive training associated with those jobs, and which often relate to guest safety. Uber has also had issues with the behavior of its drivers, and the company itself has been criticized for exploiting its drivers. Uber is facing several legal cases in the United States and was temporarily banned in London in late 2017 over concerns for user safety. In Japan, some local governments have introduced regulations that limit Airbnb operations, such as only allowing weekend operations in residential areas in certain cities.

Uber is another dominant application that is creating a lot of disruption in the taxi business.

One key question for the sharing economy is whether the service providers are employees of the companies or not. This must be decided on a case by case basis, and will have a huge impact on the lives of the service providers and on how sharing economy businesses are operated.

7 The sharing economy seems set to expand and is here to stay. Thousands of businesses, cities, and customers are enjoying the benefits of the sharing economy. The sharing economy and "traditional" business have a difficult relationship, though, and time will tell how this relationship develops as different countries around the world decide how the sharing economy should be regulated. In the meantime, it is hard to deny the huge benefits that the sharing economy is bringing to millions of people everywhere.

Chapter 11 **Uber, Airbnb, and TaskRabbit** – *Collaborative Consumption and the Sharing Economy*

NOTES ··

collaborative consumption「協調的消費」　**sharing economy**「シェアリングエコミー, 共有（型）経済」　**Bank of America**「バンク・オブ・アメリカ」米国の大手商業銀行　**carsharing**「カーシェアリング」自動車を複数の会員で共同利用するシステム。短時間・短距離の利用であれば、レンタカーよりも割安になることが多い。レンタカーのように店頭での手続きがなく、スマートフォンなどを使用してネットで予約できる。　**carpooling**「カープーリング」自家用車の相乗り　**Airbnb**「エアビーアンドビー」　**listing**「（登録された）物件」　**property**「不動産物件」　**villa**「ビラ」田舎や郊外の堂々とした邸宅・別荘　**yurt**「ユルト」モンゴルの遊牧民の居住する円形型移動テント　**igloo**「イグルー」カナダのイヌイットの住居にみられるドーム型の家　**Uber**「ウーバー」米国の配車サービス大手企業　**account**「アカウント」インターネットやＥメールを利用する際に、ユーザー名（＝ ID）とパスワードで構築される、その利用者を認識する文字情報。ユーザー名をアカウントとも呼ぶ。　**auto-rickshaw**「自動三輪車」　**party**「当事者,関係者」　**Ikea**「イケア」スウェーデン発祥の世界最大級の家具製造・販売店　**tourist destination**「観光（目的）地」　**CogiCogi**「コギコギ」　**ShareNori**「シェアのり」　**disruption**「混乱」　**exploit**「搾取する」　**seem set to ~**「～する見通しだ」　**(be) here to stay**「定着している」

Questions for Understanding

Part 1 *Look at the following statements. Write T if the statement is true, and F if it is false. Write the number of the paragraph where you find the answer in the parenthesis.*

1. The sharing economy has existed for a long time.

   T/F ____
   (# ____)

2. You can stay on a boat or in a castle using Airbnb.

   T/F ____
   (# ____)

3. Uber has created over 50 billionaires since its founding.

   T/F ____
   (# ____)

4. TaskRabbit guarantees customer satisfaction.

   T/F ____
   (# ____)

Part 2 *Look at the questions below. Check the best answer for each.*

1. How many customers has Airbnb had since it started?
   a. ☐ 4 million　b. ☐ 200 million　c. ☐ 50 billion　d. ☐ 1 million

2. What does the Uber application not do?
   a. ☐ Match drivers and customers
   b. ☐ Handle reviews and payments
   c. ☐ Establish trust between the parties
   d. ☐ Train the drivers

3. What did Kamaishi City decide to do?
   a. ☐ Create its own taxi service
   b. ☐ Start investing a lot of money in hotels
   c. ☐ Experiment with the sharing economy
   d. ☐ Renovate many farmhouses and community spaces

4. What is a major issue with companies like Airbnb and Uber?
   a. ☐ They sometimes only operate at weekends.
   b. ☐ Unregulated businesses can create danger for customers.
   c. ☐ Hosts and drivers are badly behaved.
   d. ☐ Companies refuse to pay their workers properly.

Summary

② 09

Fill each space with the best word or phrase from the list below.

properties	exploit	transform	regulation	collaborative
time will tell				

While the tendency to share has existed for a long time, the sharing or 1) _____ economy is the result of recent technological advances. Various new companies such as Airbnb and Uber have enabled people to make money from their 2) _____ and their cars. It is true to say that the sharing economy has the power to 3) _____ the world and it is projected to be worth $2 trillion by 2025. There are, however, challenges that remain such as the lack of 4) _____ of these new businesses and worries about customer safety. There is also concern that some of these new businesses may 5) _____ their workers. 6) _____ how these issues will be resolved.

60

What do YOU think?

Choose ONE of the statements below. Do you agree or disagree with it? Why? Prepare a short response giving your opinion.

▶ Companies like Airbnb must be regulated in Japan in order to protect public safety.

▶ If I have the chance, I would like to try working in the sharing economy.

Uber is redefining the transportation industry now; Airbnb is doing it to the hotel industry. You can expect that to happen in every single industry.

Masayoshi Son (1957-)
Chairman and CEO of Softbank Group

Chapter 12
More Than eMoney
What Is the Blockchain?

Useful Words

Choose a word from the list below to complete each sentence.

1. The restaurant received a booking for a _____ of four.
2. Some companies use _____ messaging apps for security purposes.
3. Magicians should never _____ how they do their tricks.
4. Many businesses _____ many tasks, saving time and money.
5. Unfortunately, many cases of credit card _____ are reported every day.

| party | automate | reveal | fraud | encrypted |

Reading

1 The word "blockchain" has become very familiar in recent times. In the simplest terms, a blockchain is something that enables the sharing of encrypted information on a closed network. It can be thought of as a ledger (a kind of list) of transactions between different parties within that network. For example, it can be used for a simple payment. If person A pays person B a certain amount of money, this transaction will be represented in a "block." The block is then verified by copying it onto a large number of computers that use mathematical software to create a unique number for that block. Since many computers have copies of the block and its unique number, it is almost impossible to change it. This process is repeated each time the block is used in a different transaction, creating a chain of verified transactions — thus the name Blockchain.

2 The blockchain system was invented in 2008 by Satoshi Nakamoto when he was developing the digital currency known as Bitcoin. The system underlying a blockchain is called distributed ledger technology, and it allows a network to agree on the correctness of a blockchain at regular intervals. Once verified by the network and recorded in the blockchain, a transaction can never be changed or deleted. It is a secure, permanent, and transparent record. It also provides a certain amount of anonymity for the users: their identities are not revealed but there is an identity number attached to each transaction. As a result, a blockchain does not require a central authority, and the parties involved do not have to trust each other. While Bitcoin is the most famous example of how the technology is used, its capabilities extend far beyond digital currencies.

3 There are many potential uses for this technology. For example, it can have applications in logistics systems. Companies such as United Parcel Service (UPS) and Walmart are developing blockchains to automate the movement of goods in order to cut costs and increase reliability. Blockchains are also being developed in the travel industry, for national voting systems, for government tax collection, leasing

Kolin Burges protests in front of the former headquarters of Mt. Gox after it suddenly closed in 2014. It was the biggest Bitcoin virtual exchange in the world at the time.

satellites, recording intellectual property rights, and for contracts in the construction industry. Furthermore, in 2018, the city of Taipei in Taiwan announced that it intends to become a smart city using blockchains. It will create special ID cards to reduce identity theft and create a system of sensors to inform residents about various things including temperature and pollution levels. Blockchain technology is also set to help the "unbanked." Nearly 2 billion people around the world lack digital access to a bank account or financial institution. In September 2017, the government of Finland began to create a digital money system for refugees, using a credit card which does not require a central bank. The blockchain creates a new financial system and brings life-changing benefits to these people. There is hardly an area of life that blockchain technology does not have the potential to touch. In 2018 in Japan, a group of 61 banks, working with the blockchain company Ripple, developed a new blockchain-based payment app called Money Tap.

4 Despite the wide awareness and the considerable effort going into blockchain technology, it is still in its infancy, and challenges remain. For example, it takes roughly 10 minutes to confirm a transaction, which is a problem if millions or billions of transactions are involved. The technology is also unregulated, and many worry that blockchains and digital currencies could be a way for criminals and terrorists to operate secretly.

The most well-known application of blockchain technology is Bitcoin and other cryptocurrencies. The applications for this technology extend far beyond currencies, though.

5 There is also concern about security. Because the blockchain system means that data cannot be changed and each block is verified by many different computers on a network, it is very secure. This means that contracts created using blockchains, often called "smart contracts," are safer because they reduce the chance of error or fraud. As a result, many companies and governments are starting to use blockchains as ways to prevent identity theft, to keep the Internet of Things secure, and to replace passwords.

6 However, while blockchains seem to be very secure, the same cannot be said of the digital currencies that use them. Several high-profile thefts have occurred. In Hong Kong in 2016, hackers stole $72 million in Bitcoin from the Bitfinex exchange. In Japan in 2014, hackers stole 700,000 Bitcoins worth $473 million from the Mt. Gox digital currency trading company. Also in Japan, in 2018, hackers stole $534.8 million of the NEM digital currency from another digital currency trading company, Coincheck. However, because blockchains guarantee anonymity, it is very difficult to discover who the thieves were. These kinds of incidents reduce people's trust in the new technology.

7 Blockchains are going to become an increasingly important part of our lives. As they become more mainstream, and the various challenges are overcome, it is possible that everyone on the planet may end up being touched by a blockchain in some way. The arrival of blockchains could change the way we use money and do business and will likely disrupt some industries as they grow in popularity. It remains to be seen exactly what changes blockchains will bring.

| | Chapter 12 | **More Than eMoney** — *What Is the Blockchain?* |

NOTES

blockchain「ブロックチェーン」金融取引などの記録をコンピューターネットワーク上で管理する技術の1つ。取引情報を複数のコンピューターで共有して検証し、正しい記録を一定量（ブロック）ごとにまとめて鎖（チェーン）のようにつないで蓄積する。　**encrypted**「暗号化された」　**ledger**「台帳」　**transaction**「取引」　**verify**「検証・承認する」　**digital currency**「デジタル通貨」　**distributed ledger technology**「分散型台帳技術」　**delete**「削除・消去する」　**anonymity**「匿名性」　**central authority**「中央当局」ここでは中央銀行や金融政策を担う中央省庁を指す。　**capabilities**「（適用・発展の）可能性」　**logistics system**「物流システム」　**United Parcel Service (UPS)** ※ Chapter 7 を参照　**Walmart**「ウォルマート」米国のスーパーマーケットチェーン大手　**intellectual property right**「知的財産権」　**identity theft**「個人情報の盗難」　**infancy**「初期段階」　**Internet of Things** ※ Chapter 5 を参照　**high-profile**「注目を浴びる」　**Bitfinex exchange**「ビットフィネックス取引所」香港を拠点とする仮想通貨の大手取引所

Questions for Understanding

Part 1 *Look at the following statements. Write T if the statement is true, and F if it is false. Write the number of the paragraph where you find the answer in the parenthesis.*

1. A transaction recorded in a blockchain is impossible to change.

   T/F
   (#　　　)

2. Blockchains require a central authority to confirm the transaction.

   T/F
   (#　　　)

3. According to the passage, Taipei is using Ripple to become a smart city.

   T/F
   (#　　　)

4. The Coincheck incident shows how anonymity increases trust in this new technology.

   T/F
   (#　　　)

Part 2 *Look at the questions below. Check the best answer for each.*

1. Who does the "unbanked" in paragraph 3 refer to?
   [Blockchain technology is also set to help the "<u>unbanked</u>."]
   a. ☐ People with no money
   b. ☐ People with no access to the banking system
   c. ☐ People who can no longer access their bank accounts
   d. ☐ People who can only access digital currencies

65

2. How is the government of Finland helping refugees?
   a. ☐ It is issuing credit cards to them.
   b. ☐ It is opening bank accounts for them.
   c. ☐ It is helping them use digital currencies.
   d. ☐ It is training them to develop blockchains.

3. What is a major concern regarding blockchain technology?
   a. ☐ The cost of each transaction
   b. ☐ The need for complicated passwords
   c. ☐ The need to verify IDs
   d. ☐ The time it takes to process a transaction

4. What might happen in the future in regard to blockchain technology?
   a. ☐ It might disappear due to security concerns.
   b. ☐ It might touch everyone in some way.
   c. ☐ It might only be used by high-tech companies
   d. ☐ It might be only be used by governments.

Summary

② 17

Fill each space with the best word from the list below.

reliability	applications	logistics	term	high-profile	currency

The 1) _____ "blockchain" has become very familiar in recent years. A digital 2) _____ created using blockchain technology, called Bitcoin, has been widely covered in the media. The blockchain, however, has many other 3) _____, and its use in smart contracts is being examined in many industries. In particular, it seems to have a lot of potential in the 4) _____ business, and companies like UPS and Walmart are making fast progress in this area. As the 5) _____ of the systems increase, and the level of trust increases, it is possible that one day the blockchain will feature in our daily lives. For now, some concerns remain and 6) _____ thefts and fraud continue to make people doubt whether it can truly work.

66

More Than eMoney – *What Is the Blockchain?*

What do YOU think?

Choose ONE of the statements below. Do you agree or disagree with it? Why? Prepare a short response giving your opinion.

▶ The blockchain may be useful, but many people in Japan prefer to use cash instead of digital money.

▶ The digital currencies created by the blockchain will one day replace national currencies.

> *The blockchain is the financial challenge of our time. It is going to change the way that our financial world operates.*
>
> Blythe Masters (1969-)
> CEO of Digital Asset Holdings

Chapter 13

Permanently Part-Time

Is the Gig Economy the Future of Work?

Useful Words

Choose a word or phrase from the list below to complete each sentence.

1. Scientific knowledge is _____ knowledge; it is revised when new discoveries are made.

2. Instead of two terms each year, the university decided to _____ a three-semester system from 2020.

3. Anyone who is born in the United States has the right to become a U.S. _____.

4. I prefer to study alone because I can't _____ my work if other people are talking.

5. As my phone service is expensive and unreliable, I think I will change my _____.

| service provider | focus on | contingent | adopt | citizen |

Reading

1 For most of human history, the majority of people have focused on one kind of work above all others, producing food. Until the middle of the 19th century, around 80 percent of people were involved in agriculture. However, things changed rapidly during the Industrial Revolution, when new technology that allowed more
5 food to be produced by fewer people was developed. By 1900, the proportion of people who were involved in agriculture in industrialized countries like Britain and the United States had fallen to around 30 percent. By 2000, this figure had fallen to about 2 percent of workers. Instead of working on farms in the countryside, many people moved to the cities and took jobs working in factories producing new goods

and products, or took service jobs, such as in shops, offices, schools, and restaurants.

2 As with agriculture in the 19th century, new technology was also applied to manufacturing during the 20th century. As a result, the proportion of people working in factories fell from about 50 percent in 1900 to about 10 percent in 2000, and the proportion of people doing service jobs increased. Today, new technologies, especially advances in robotics and artificial intelligence, are enabling the service industry to achieve more with fewer people. Consequently, instead of full-time jobs more and more people have found themselves doing contingent jobs, that is, part-time, temporary, or contract jobs. This is often referred to as the "gig economy." In 2015, the U.S. Government Accountability Office found that 40.4 percent of American workers were contingent workers. In the same year, 24 percent of British workers and 22.7 percent of Japanese workers were contingent workers, compared to the OECD average of 16.8 percent.

How can you earn the money you need?

3 Perhaps the company that best illustrates the gig economy is Uber. The Uber smartphone app allows its users to call for a driver when they need to travel. However, unlike a regular taxi, Uber drivers use their own cars. The cost of the journey is decided by Uber, based on the time of day and the length of the journey, and both the driver and the passenger can rate each other via the app. Uber has become extremely popular since it began in 2009. In 2017, it had more than 1.5 million drivers, was available in 83 countries, and served more than 40 million customers a month. However, Uber is not alone, there are many other companies providing an online service to connect customers and workers, including Airbnb, TaskRabbit, and Etsy. This part of the gig economy, the use of the Internet, social media, and smartphone apps to connect customers with service providers, is sometimes referred to as the "sharing economy." For customers, these companies are convenient and easy to use, while the service providers can earn more money and have a working day that is very flexible.

4 So will we all be working in the gig economy soon? There are definitely some benefits to contingent work. As well as the flexibility in work hours, these jobs provide a range of work experience, and also allow workers to find out if a particular kind of job suits them. However, contingent workers have little job security, rarely receive the same benefits as full-time staff, and do not benefit from the same salary structure. In other words, they can be fired at any time, do not get health and pension benefits, and can earn as little as a third of the salary of a full-time worker doing the same job.

Will everybody have this choice in the future?

5 Is it possible to avoid the problems related to contingent work? One possible answer is a universal basic income (UBI). A UBI is money that is paid to every citizen of a country, whether they are rich or poor. This money would replace any existing welfare payments, such as unemployment insurance or pensions, and would allow people to live a comfortable life even if they did not work. This is not a new idea, it was first suggested in the United States in 1797 by Thomas Paine in his book *Agrarian Justice*. However, the idea was not tested until the 1960s. In 2017, while no country had fully adopted the idea of a UBI, several countries were testing it, including Canada, Finland, Kenya, the Netherlands, and Uganda. While the evidence from most UBI trials is positive, that is, most people receiving a UBI continued working, stayed in education, or took part in volunteer activities, many people remain unconvinced by the idea. In fact, 77 percent of the people of Switzerland voted against a UBI when the idea was suggested in 2016.

6 It seems likely the development of new technologies will result in more and more of us working in the gig economy instead of traditional full-time jobs. The greatest risk is that people will find themselves permanently doing low-paid, unsatisfying part-time jobs. One possible solution is to implement a UBI, but there may be other ways for governments to insure that the citizens of their countries are able to live comfortable lives and to do meaningful work. This is the challenge that the gig economy poses.

Chapter 13　**Permanently Part-Time** *– Is the Gig Economy the Future of Work?*

NOTES

the Industrial Revolution「産業革命」18 世紀後半から 19 世紀前半にかけて、英国での急速・連続的な技術革新に伴う社会・経済上の大変革。この革命は 19 世紀から 20 世紀初めにかけて他の欧米諸国や日本に波及した。　**artificial intelligence** (= AI)「人工知能（AI）」　**gig economy**「ギグエコノミー」インターネットを通じて単発・短期の仕事を受発注する働き方や、そのような非正規労働によって成り立つ経済形態　**U.S. Government Accountability Office**「米政府監査院」連邦予算の支出や政府機関の内外での活動を監査し、議会に報告する。　**contingent worker**「非正規労働者」　**OECD** ※ Chapter 4 を参照　**Etsy**「エッツィ」個人が手作りした商品やビンテージ品を販売・購入できる米国のオンライン販売サイト　**sharing economy** ※ Chapter 11 を参照　**job security**「雇用の保障」　**salary structure**「給与体系」　**health and pension benefits**「健康保険補助と年金給付」　**universal basic income (UBI)**「最低所得保障」　**unemployment insurance**「失業保険」　**Thomas Paine**「トマス・ペイン」英国出身の米国の哲学者（1737-1809）　***Agrarian Justice***『農民の正義』

Questions for Understanding

Part 1　*Look at the following statements. Write T if the statement is true, and F if it is false. Write the number of the paragraph where you find the answer in the parenthesis.*

1. These days, the majority of workers in industrialized countries have service jobs.
T/F　
(#　　)

2. The main cause for changes in work is the development of new technologies.
T/F　
(#　　)

3. According to the passage, everyone will have a part-time job in the future.
T/F　
(#　　)

4. The universal basic income was first tested more than 200 years ago.
T/F　
(#　　)

Part 2　*Look at the questions below. Check the best answer for each.*

1. What proportion of people in industrialized countries worked in agriculture in 2000?
    a. ☐ 2%　　　　b. ☐ 10%　　　　c. ☐ 30%　　　　d. ☐ 80%

2. According to the OECD, what proportion of workers in Japan are contingent workers?
    a. ☐ Nearly one in two　　　　b. ☐ Nearly one in three
    c. ☐ Nearly one in four　　　　d. ☐ Nearly one in five

71

3. Choose the word that has the closest meaning to "unconvinced" in the following sentence in Paragraph 5.

   While the evidence from most UBI trials is positive, that is, most people receiving a UBI continued working, stayed in education, or took part in volunteer activities, many people remain <u>unconvinced</u> by the idea.

   a. ☐ concerned   **b.** ☐ doubtful   **c.** ☐ pleased   **d.** ☐ unaffected

4. Which countries are testing a universal basic income?
   a. ☐ Canada, Finland, Kenya, the Netherlands, Switzerland
   b. ☐ Canada, Finland, Kenya, Switzerland, Uganda
   c. ☐ Canada, Finland, Kenya, the Netherlands, Uganda
   d. ☐ the United States, Finland, Kenya, the Netherlands, Uganda

Summary

② 24

Fill each space with the best word from the list below.

allow (someone to)	robotics	consequently	temporary
pensions	evidence		

The relationship between technology and work has always been complex. Generally, as one new technology replaces people doing one kind of work, another creates new jobs for them to do. 1) _____, over the last 200 years, the majority of jobs have moved from agriculture to manufacturing to service industries. However, one thing was constant: people could always find full-time jobs. The development of the Internet and 2) _____ may have broken that pattern. Does this mean that the future of work will be limited to 3) _____ or part-time jobs? If so, what will happen to the traditional benefits of full-time work, such as healthcare and 4) _____? One possible solution is the universal basic income, an income everyone receives — whether they need it or not. While some people may object to giving people "money for nothing," the 5) _____ indicates that the universal basic income can 6) _____ people to study, start businesses, and to volunteer.

Chapter 13 **Permanently Part-Time** *– Is the Gig Economy the Future of Work?*

What do YOU think?

Choose ONE of the statements below. Do you agree or disagree with it? Why?
Prepare a short response giving your opinion.

> ▶ The development of businesses like Uber will have a bad effect on society.
>
> ▶ Japan should introduce the universal basic income.

Nothing is really work unless you would rather be doing something else.

J. M. Barrie (1860-1937)

Scottish author

73

Chapter 14

Driven to Succeed

The Amazing Story of Elon Musk

Useful Words

Choose a word from the list below to complete each sentence.

1. The best teachers _____ us to become the best we can be.

2. _____ thinking often prevents us from seeing the solution to a problem.

3. The _____ goal in life for many people is to be happy.

4. Many children dream of becoming an _____, and going into space.

5. Some governments _____ the rights and freedoms of their people.

> conventional   astronaut   ultimate   oppress   challenge

Reading

② 25~30

25

1 Elon Musk is a man who has re-invented industries, challenged conventional thinking, solved "unsolvable" problems, and wants to change the future of humanity. Born in South Africa, Musk was interested in technology from an early age. In 1984, when he was 12, he wrote a computer game called Blastar. In 1995, after moving to
5   the United States, he and his brother started a company called Zip2, which helped people to find local companies on the Internet. In 1999, he sold Zip2, making a profit of $22 million. He then invested in a company that provided online financial services, and which eventually became Paypal. When eBay bought Paypal for $1.5 billion in 2002, Musk earned $156 million. Elon Musk has also started several more
10   companies with the potential to change our world and how we live, including Tesla,

74

which makes electric vehicles, SpaceX, which builds rockets for space travel, and SolarCity, which is the largest provider of solar power in the U.S.

2 Musk is perhaps best known for his electric car company, Tesla. Getting Tesla's first car, the Roadster, into production in 2008 almost bankrupted him. However, the car Tesla created, the world's first luxury electric sports car, was truly groundbreaking. By 2018, the Tesla Model S, the Model X, and the Model 3 had also been released, and Tesla had made more than 300,000 cars. In addition, Tesla also makes electric engines for Daimler and Toyota.

3 SpaceX was founded in 2002, and its aim is "to revolutionize space technology, with the ultimate goal of enabling people to live on other planets." One way it tries to do this is by making its spacecraft and rockets reusable, cutting the cost of space travel dramatically. SpaceX was the first private company to successfully return a spacecraft from low-earth orbit. SpaceX has also pioneered returning booster rockets to their bases so they can be recycled.

"Starman" drives a Tesla Roadster into space as part of SpaceX's Falcon Heavy rocket launch in early 2018

When SpaceX first did this in 2015, it achieved something that even national space agencies like NASA and JAXA had not been able to do. Since 2008, SpaceX has had a contract with NASA to use the SpaceX Falcon 9 rocket and Dragon spacecraft to take supplies to the International Space Station, and is planning the next step: taking astronauts into space. In February 2018, SpaceX launched its Falcon Heavy rocket. The Falcon Heavy is currently the most powerful rocket in the world, and the fourth-most powerful rocket ever built. It is designed to take astronauts to the Moon and, eventually, to Mars. However, the first launch contained a Tesla Roadster "driven" by a dummy astronaut named Starman.

4 SolarCity aims to provide affordable solar power in order to help reduce the effects of climate change. SolarCity makes various kinds of solar panels, including some that look like regular roof tiles. This allows the whole roof of a house to generate solar power. However, simply generating solar power is not enough, because the sun goes down at night. Consequently, the solar power generated during the day is stored in a battery called a Powerwall so that the home has power through the night. Larger versions of the Powerwall battery, called the Powerpack, also exist. For example, in 2017, SolarCity built a 13 megawatt solar power farm, with a 52 megawatt battery system on the Hawaiian island of Kauai. Also in 2017, the government of South Australia installed 100 megawatts of Powerpack batteries — enough to power 30,000 homes — after Elon Musk promised that Tesla could produce them within 100 days. Why did he do that? The reason was that Tesla had had some problems making enough cars for the people that wanted them. By doing this, Elon Musk showed the world that Tesla could be relied on to keep its promises.

This huge American solar farm provides power for thousands of homes.

5 Despite his successes in the fields of electric vehicles, spacecraft, and solar power, Elon Musk has not finished. In 2013, he announced his interest in developing a super-fast public transportation system called the Hyperloop. In 2015, he announced the creation of OpenAI, a non-profit company that will research artificial intelligence in order to, "counteract large corporations who may gain too much power by owning superintelligence systems devoted to profits, as well as governments which may use AI to gain power and even oppress their citizenry." In 2016, he co-founded Neuralink, a company designed to find ways to connect human brains and artificial intelligence.

6 What are the keys to his success? The first is a strong belief that it is his purpose to make the world a better place. Secondly, he has been willing to throw his entire effort into these goals and take huge risks in the process. His determination and ability to drive down costs has changed both the automotive and space industries. Thirdly, he has the quality of resilience. Musk continues to defy his critics and to recast industries while making amazing advances. The world clearly needs more people like Elon Musk. Perhaps reading his story will inspire you to go out and pursue your own world-changing ambitions.

Chapter 14	**Driven to Succeed** – *The Amazing Story of Elon Musk*

NOTES

conventional「従来型の」 **Paypal**「ペイパル」インターネットを利用した決済サービス。世界で2億人以上が利用している。 **eBay**「イーベイ」米国のインターネット競売を中心としたサービスを提供するウェブサイト **Daimler**「ダイムラー社」ドイツの自動車メーカー。乗用車メルセデス・ベンツなどを製造・販売。 **low-earth orbit**「地球（周回）低軌道」 **booster rocket**「打ち上げロケット」 **NASA** (= National Aeronautics and Space Administration)「（米）航空宇宙局」 **JAXA** (= Japan Aerospace Exploration Agency)「（日本の）宇宙航空研究開発機構」 **International Space Station**「国際宇宙ステーション」米国、ロシア、欧州諸国、日本、カナダの15カ国が共同運用する有人宇宙施設。搭乗員は6人。軌道高度約420キロの宇宙環境で研究・実験を行っている。 **Falcon Heavy**「ファルコンヘビー」全長70メートルの2段式大型ロケット。発射後に切り離される1段目のロケットは自動制御で地球に帰還し、回収後に再利用できる。 **Mars**「火星」 **Tesla Roadstar** 米電気自動車メーカー「テスラ」のスポーツカー「ロードスター」 **dummy**「模型の」 **Starman**『スターマン』英国のロック歌手デヴィッド・ボウイ(1947-2016) が作詞・作曲し1972年にリリースされた楽曲。この曲の中には、"There's a starman waiting in the sky" という一節がある。 **megawatt**「メガワット」1 megawatt (MW) = 1,000 kilowatt (kW)。発電所の電力の単位として、日本の新聞や電力会社は一般にキロワットを使用している。1,000キロワット以上の出力の大規模太陽光発電所（メガソーラー）が建設されるようになり、メガワットも使用されている。 **South Australia**「サウスオーストラリア州」オーストラリア中南部の州。 **Hyperloop**「ハイパールーブ」低圧状態に保たれたチューブ内を列車が浮遊した状態で、空気抵抗を受けずに超高速で運行する輸送システム。 **counteract**「（〜の力に）対抗する」 **superintelligence**「スーパーインテリジェンス，超絶知能」人類の知力の総和を超越する能力を持つ人工知能、またはその能力を備えた機械。 **citizenry**「（集合的に）市民」一般市民全体を指す。 **resilience**「立ち直る力」 **defy**「反抗する；無視する」 **critic**「批判する人」 **recast**「再編成する；作り直す」

Questions for Understanding

Part 1 *Look at the following statements. Write T if the statement is true, and F if it is false. Write the number of the paragraph where you find the answer in the parenthesis.*

1. Elon Musk made most of his early money from selling computer games.

   T/F
   (#   )

2. Tesla makes cars for other car companies such as Daimler and Toyota.

   T/F
   (#   )

3. The Falcon Heavy rocket left Earth for its journey to Mars in 2018.

   T/F
   (#   )

4. According to the passage, the Powerwall is simply a big battery.

   T/F
   (#   )

77

Part 2 *Look at the questions below. Check the best answer for each.*

1. What is the correct order for these events in Elon Musk's early life?
   a. ☐ Writes Blastar → Sells Zip 2 → eBay buys Paypal
   b. ☐ Sells Zip 2 → eBay buys Paypal → Writes Blastar
   c. ☐ Writes Blastar → eBay buys Paypal → Sells Zip 2
   d. ☐ Sells Zip 2 → Writes Blastar → eBay buys Paypal

2. What is a key characteristic of SpaceX?
   a. ☐ Its ability to absorb large costs
   b. ☐ Its ability to cut huge costs
   c. ☐ Its ability to recruit staff from NASA
   d. ☐ Its ability to launch cars into space

3. Why did Elon Musk make his 100-day promise to the government of South Australia?
   a. ☐ He needed to make quick sales.
   b. ☐ He wanted to show off.
   c. ☐ He wanted to show he could be relied on.
   d. ☐ He wanted to test the Powerpack factory equipment.

4. What other areas of business is Elon Musk interested in?
   a. ☐ Public transportation and the human brain
   b. ☐ Computer games and online auctions
   c. ☐ Internet development and human resources
   d. ☐ Digital music and financial services

Chapter 14   **Driven to Succeed** – *The Amazing Story of Elon Musk*

Summary

② 31

Fill each space with the best word from the list below.

determination   generated   groundbreaking   affordable   defy   pioneered

Elon Musk's adventures in business have been truly 1) _____.
He has 2) _____ the development of electric car technology, and
3) _____ space rockets and solar panels with his companies
Tesla, SpaceX, and SolarCity. Many thought the technical challenges
behind the success of these companies could not be overcome. Musks's
4) _____ to succeed has enabled him to 5) _____ his
critics. He has 6) _____ huge interest in his ventures and managed to
make a personal fortune in the process. Making money was never the primary
goal for him though; his aim is to change the course of human history.

What do YOU think?

Choose ONE of the statements below. Do you agree or disagree with it? Why?
Prepare a short response giving your opinion.

▶ Business is not about saving the world; it is simply about making money.
▶ Given the situation on Earth, one day we will have to leave and find other places
to live such as on Mars.

....

....

....

....

> *Life needs to be more than just solving everyday problems. You*
> *need to wake up and be excited about the future.*
>
> Elon Musk (1971-)
> South African-born entrepreneur

79

Chapter 15: The Clanking Masses
Will a Robot Take Your Job?

Useful Words

Choose a word from the list below to complete each sentence.

1. We heard a _____ noise when we started the old machine.
2. Leonardo Da Vinci is credited with the original _____ of the helicopter.
3. If you focus on learning something for a long time, _____ you will become a master.
4. Social _____ is very important for children at school.
5. With _____ resources, a company can attempt some very ambitious projects.

| clanking | sufficient | eventually | interaction | invention |

Reading

1 The word "robot" comes from the Czech word "robota," which describes a kind of slavery. The word was first used in the title of the 1920 Czech play *R.U.R.* (*Rossum's Universal Robots*). The play is about the invention of robots and how the robots eventually destroy humanity. While the idea of robots destroying humanity and taking over the world is common in science fiction, it does not seem likely to happen. However, while your life may be safe from the robots, your job may not be.

2 Dramatic advances in robotics and artificial intelligence (AI) are rapidly transforming our lives. In 1997, IBM's Deep Blue computer beat the world champion chess player, Garry Kasparov. Just 20 years later, Google's AI program, Alpha Go, beat the best go player in the world, Ke Jie. The same program also taught itself to play chess to an unbeatable level in only four hours. While winning some games may not seem to be an important achievement, chess and go are perhaps the most complex games invented. Furthermore, the ability to learn rules and respond effectively to another person's actions can be applied to many different tasks.

A picture of a man being defeated by a machine. Garry Kasparov, the reigning Chess World Champion at the time, loses to Deep Blue in the famous games of 1997.

3 Robots have been replacing humans in the manufacturing industry for many years, but they are now entering a wide variety of other industries, too. For example, most large automobile companies, from Ford to Toyota, are developing driverless vehicle technology. By 2016, Google's driverless cars had driven more than 2,777,585 kilometers on roads in the United States. While driverless cars may be convenient, what about the people who drive for a living? In Japan alone, there are more than 250,000 taxi drivers, and more than 1 million truckers. If they are replaced by driverless vehicles, what will they do instead?

4 The history of industry shows us that when machines replace humans in one kind of job, they can usually find jobs in a different industrial sector. For example, farm workers took jobs in factories, and then factory workers took jobs in the service industry. Unlike mining, farming, or manufacturing, service industries do not produce products. Instead, service industries connect customers with products or provide a service as a product which is intangible. For example, people working in shops and restaurants are working in the service industry, as are teachers, lawyers, and doctors. In many countries, the service industry is now the largest industrial sector. In 2017, 80.2 percent of U.S. workers had jobs in the service industry. In the same year in Japan, it was 69.3 percent.

5 The service industry relies on human interaction, i.e. people talking to each other. Natural conversation is currently something that robots cannot achieve. It is easy to confuse Apple's Siri or Amazon's Alexa, for example. However, the ability of a robot to have a conversation is constantly being improved, and for some tasks a limited ability is sufficient. When we telephone a call center or helpline, many of us already talk to an AI system initially, and in some cases, we may never actually talk to a person at all. Furthermore, most of our online shopping experiences are done using computers rather than people. But why replace people with machines? The main reason is that people are expensive to employ, while machines are cheaper. In 2017, in Japan, the Fukoku Mutual Life Insurance Company decided to replace 34 staff members with AI designed by IBM. It expects to save about $1.2 million per year by using the new system.

Sophia is one of the most advanced robots on the planet and is the first robot to become a citizen of a country — Saudi Arabia.

6 For some jobs, a robot is clearly superior. However, for the most complex jobs, such as in medicine, research has shown that people working together with AI get the best results. It is estimated that robots and AI will take over about 5 million jobs in the world's richest countries by 2025. But this may not be a disaster. In farming and manufacturing, machines have taken over most of the dirty and dangerous jobs. In the service industry, they are taking over the dull ones. Perhaps the AI and robot revolution will free us to do the kinds of jobs we enjoy and help us to do them better.

NOTES

R.U.R. (Rossum's Universal Robots) 『ロッサム・ユニバーサル・ロボット会社』チェコの作家カレル・チャペックの戯曲。感情を持つロボットが登場する。　***Garry Kasparov*** 「ガルリ・カスパロフ（1963-）」チェスの元世界王者。ロシア生まれで、22歳から15年間にわたり王座を保持した。　***Alpha Go*** 「アルファ碁」グーグル傘下のAI開発ベンチャー「ディープマインド」（英国）が開発した囲碁のAIプログラム。ニューラルネットワークによる自己学習能力で自らを強化することができ、プロ棋士に勝利を収めた。　***Ke Jie*** 「柯潔」中国人棋士（九段）　***mining industry*** 「鉱業」　***service industry*** 「サービス産業」物財の生産を主とする産業に対し、サービスそのものの提供を主とする産業の総称。総務省が実施する「サービス産業動向調査」の調査対象となっているのは、日本標準産業分類のうちの次の産業。①情報通信業②運輸・郵便業③不動産・物品賃貸業④学術研

Chapter 15   **The Clanking Masses** – *Will a Robot Take Your Job?*

究、専門・技術サービス業⑤宿泊・飲食サービス業⑥生活関連サービス・娯楽業⑦教育、学習支援業⑧医療、福祉⑨他に分類されないサービス業　**intangible**「無形の」　**i.e.** (= id est　ラテン語)「すなわち，言い換えれば (= that is)」　**helpline**「電話相談窓口」　**Fukoku Mutual Insurance Company**「富国生命保険相互会社」略称はフコク生命。

Questions for Understanding

Part 1   *Look at the following statements. Write T if the statement is true, and F if it is false. Write the number of the paragraph where you find the answer in the parenthesis.*

1. *Rossum's Universal Robots* is about how robots steal jobs from people working in offices.

    T/F
    (#   )

2. Machines can now master advanced strategy games in a few hours.

    T/F
    (#   )

3. Machines are already dominating jobs in the service industry.

    T/F
    (#   )

4. Robots are not capable of having a natural conversation.

    T/F
    (#   )

Part 2   *Look at the questions below. Check the best answer for each.*

1. Why is the computer Deep Blue important?
   a. ☐ It was the first computer to play chess at a high level.
   b. ☐ It was the first computer to play go at a high level.
   c. ☐ It was the first computer to beat a human chess champion.
   d. ☐ It was the first computer to beat a human go champion.

2. Which of the following companies is not developing driverless car technology?
   a. ☐ Toyota   b. ☐ IBM   c. ☐ Google   d. ☐ Ford

3. What happened in Fukoku Mutual Life Insurance Company in 2017?
   a. ☐ It opened an advanced call center.
   b. ☐ It sacked all its staff members.
   c. ☐ It went bankrupt.
   d. ☐ It replaced some of its employees with robots.

4. What changes could we see take place by 2025?
   a. ☐ Five million robots will be used to do various dangerous jobs around the world.
   b. ☐ Robots will take over most office jobs.
   c. ☐ Humans and robots will work together more on complex tasks.
   d. ☐ Humans will not have many jobs left to do and will be free.

83

Summary

Fill each space with the best word from the list below.

> sector   truckers   superior   advanced   transform   achievement

The word "robot" was originally used in a Czech play in 1920, but is now a commonly used term. Robot technology has 1) _____ to a point where machines are often able to outperform their human counterparts. Deep Blue's 2) _____ of beating the world champion chess player in 1997 was a taste of things to come. AI has gone on to 3) _____ many areas of our lives. In the transportation 4) _____ for example, driverless cars are posing a challenge to human taxi drivers and 5) _____. While machines are 6) _____ in many areas, however, for the moment the most complex tasks are best achieved by humans and robots working together.

What do YOU think?

Choose ONE of the statements below. Do you agree or disagree with it? Why? Prepare a short response giving your opinion.

> ▶ Robots will eventually be able to do everything a human can do.
> ▶ It is highly likely that a robot army will one day destroy humanity.

....
....
....

> *In the twenty-first century, the robot will take the place which slave labor occupied in ancient civilization.*
>
> Nikola Tesla (1856-1943)
> Serbian American inventor and engineer

Chapter 16

It's None of Your Business!

Why Privacy Is Important

Useful Words

Choose a word or phrase from the list below to complete each sentence.

1. She spent three hours _____ in the shop before she decided which dress to buy.

2. Japan _____ one of the richest countries in the world.

3. Akane was _____ the International Circle at my university.

4. Because the pizza was delivered so late, we were told we could have it _____ .

5. Although it is unpleasant, being vaccinated is _____ to catching influenza.

preferable	in charge of	for no charge	browsing
(be) considered to be			

Reading

② 39~46

39

1 How many different ways have you used the Internet or your smartphone today? Perhaps you browsed for information, did some shopping, sent a message to a friend, contacted your bank, read a book, listened to music, shared a picture, watched a video, or played a game. The convenience and services that the Internet and our mobile devices provide us depend on two things, the free movement of ⁵ information, and keeping the data we share private and safe. However, the security and privacy of our data is under attack from four sources: companies, criminals, our governments, and ourselves. In a world where people share almost every aspect of their lives, why should privacy be something we worry about?

85

2 The English proverb that, "Your home is your castle," was first written in 1581, and became part of English law soon after. It means that neither the government, nor anybody else, has the right to interfere with your private life. This concept has been considered to be so important that it is included in the U.S. Constitution, the United Nations Universal Declaration of Human Rights, and the European Convention on Human Rights. But what exactly does your private life include?

Can YOU keep a secret?

3 Having control over your private life means having control over how you look, how you dress, your lifestyle, and your sexuality. It means that you decide who your friends will be, where you live, who can enter your home, and who can see or touch your body. Finally, it means that you control who can see or use personal information about you. However, these rights can be lost if you do something that is a crime.

4 The right to privacy can be a problem for governments. One of the duties of the government is to keep people safe from crime and terrorism. However, the right to privacy can make it difficult for the police to discover criminal plans until it is too late. This means that governments generally want to maximize surveillance of their citizens and minimize their privacy. However, many people feel that the opposite is preferable. This is because while government surveillance can be used to protect people, it can also be used to control them. Unfortunately, even though most people in government are good, some are bad, some are criminals, and some are careless. In 2018, it was discovered that some of the staff in charge of the Aadhaar database, the Indian national identity database, were selling the personal information of Indian citizens for $8 per person. Also in 2018, the government of the English city of Leicester accidentally e-mailed personal information about hundreds of children to 27 different companies.

5 Companies also want to know as much as possible about our lives so that they can sell us more of their products. Companies like Facebook and Google offer us a variety of useful and convenient services for no charge, but while we do not pay them any money, these services are not free. Instead, we pay these companies with our data, and this information is then sold to other companies so that they can focus their advertising and marketing more accurately. Criminals, on the other hand, can use the same data to steal our identities, allowing them to take out loans, get credit cards, or access our bank accounts.

6 The final threat to our privacy is ourselves. Many people are not aware of how much of their personal information they share online. Are you? For example, many users of Facebook do not change the privacy setting to limit who can see their data. This can allow anyone to share their information, or even create fake Facebook accounts using their photos, address, and phone number. For example, in Texas in 2016, bullies in a high school created fake Facebook and Twitter accounts in the name of one of their classmates. The bullying continued even after their classmate had killed herself — the bullies thought it was funny.

Is your online data safe?

7 Another problem with allowing anyone to see our personal information on the Internet is that our employers may see it. Furthermore, it is very difficult to remove something from the Internet once we have uploaded it. In fact, there are even websites, such as the Internet Archive, that are dedicated to preserving old information from the Internet. In 2018, Toby Young, a British journalist, discovered this for himself. He had been given a job with the British universities regulator, an organization which protects students studying at university. However, among the thousands of tweets he had made on Twitter since 2009, were negative comments about men of a different social class, women's bodies, and homosexuals. He had to quit after only eight days.

8 The best first step to taking control of your online privacy is to google yourself, and to then delete the information you want to get rid of, and change the privacy settings to control who can see what. You do not allow anybody to enter your home, and the same should be true of your online life. Your data is valuable and your privacy is an important right. Now is the time to protect it.

NOTES

interfere with ~「～に干渉する」　　**the United Nations Universal Declaration of Human Rights**「国連の世界人権宣言」1948年12月10日の国連総会で「全ての人民と全ての国が達成すべき人権の共通基準」として採択された。　**the European Convention on Human Rights**「欧州人権条約」世界人権宣言が定めた自由権的人権の保護を規定している地域的な人権協定。1953年に発効。　**right to privacy**「プライバシー権」私生活をみだりに公開されない権利　**surveillance**「監視」　**Aadhaar**「アドハー」ヒンディー語で「基盤」の意　**take out a loan**「ローンを組む」　**bully** (n)「いじめっ子」　**bullying**「いじめ」　**be dedicated to ~**「～に特化した」　**google** (v)「グーグルで検索する」

Questions for Understanding

Part 1 *Look at the following statements. Write T if the statement is true, and F if it is false. Write the number of the paragraph where you find the answer in the parenthesis.*

1. The idea of a private life is thought to be out of date these days.

   T/F（#　　　）

2. It can be difficult for governments to balance the right to privacy and the duty to protect people.

   T/F（#　　　）

3. Both criminals and companies want to use our data in order to make money.

   T/F（#　　　）

4. Many people do not realize how much private information they share online.

   T/F（#　　　）

Part 2 *Look at the questions below. Check the best answer for each.*

1. Choose the word that has the closest meaning to "preserving" in the following sentence in Paragraph 7.
   In fact, there are even websites, such as the Internet Archive, that are dedicated to <u>preserving</u> old information from the Internet.
   a. ☐ deleting　　b. ☐ fixing　　c. ☐ recreating　　d. ☐ saving

2. What happened in the city of Leicester?
   a. ☐ City hall staff accidentally sent private data to 27 companies.
   b. ☐ City hall staff accidentally sold private data to 27 companies.
   c. ☐ City hall staff accidentally sold private data for only $8.
   d. ☐ City hall staff accidentally sent $8 to 27 companies.

Chapter 16 **It's None of Your Business!** *– Why Privacy Is Important*

3. How do we pay for Facebook and Google services?
   - a. ☐ With a loan
   - b. ☐ With a credit card
   - c. ☐ With our data
   - d. ☐ With our bank accounts

4. What is the best first step we can take to control our data?
   - a. ☐ Delete all our information from the Internet
   - b. ☐ Only use services provided by Google
   - c. ☐ Perform an Internet search for yourself
   - d. ☐ Change the privacy settings so that anyone can see everything

Summary

② 47

Fill each space with the best word or phrase from the list below.

| surveillance | to remove | interfere with | to upload | bully | e-mail |

When you 1) _____ your friends or post a photo online, do you worry that the government might be watching? Do you worry that people who do not like you might 2) _____ your online profile in order to 3) _____ you? It is easy to forget that a lot of the Internet is public and not private. It is also easy to forget that while it is easy 4) _____ something to the Internet, it is not so simple 5) _____ it. Many of the companies that provide us with online services do not charge us money. Instead they use our data to sell advertising. As a result, it is important for us to control what data we make public. The Internet is a very powerful and useful tool, but unfortunately, some governments use it for 6) _____ and to control the citizens of their countries. It is up to us to make sure we do not become easy targets for bad governments, bullies, and criminals when we use online services.

89

What do YOU think?

Choose ONE of the statements below. Do you agree or disagree with it? Why? Prepare a short response giving your opinion.

▶ The government should be allowed to see all of our data all of the time.
▶ Online bullying is not as serious as bullying in real life.

You have zero privacy anyway. Get over it.

Scott McNealy (1954-)
Co-founder of Sun Microsystems

Chapter 17

I'll See You in Court!

What Is the Rule of Law?

Useful Words

Choose a word or phrase from the list below to complete each sentence.

1. Since she had studied so hard, she was _____ that she would pass the exam.

2. It is important for referees to be _____ and treat each team the same.

3. The new mayor and city _____ have promised to build a new sports center.

4. My 5-kilometer run should take only 30 minutes, but _____ it always takes me a little longer.

5. My little brother just wants to play all the time. If it weren't for his _____, my homework would be finished already.

| impartial | interference | in practice | confident | council |

Reading

② 48~53

48

1 In the town of Cheran, in the state of Michoacan in southern Mexico, the main industries are farming and logging trees from the local mountain. In 2011, the people discovered that gangsters were stealing the trees and that the police did nothing to stop them. Furthermore, the town's politicians ignored the peoples' complaints. As a result, the townspeople decided that they needed neither corrupt police nor 5 politicians, and on April 15, 2011, they forced them out of the town. In their place, a new town council and militia (a group of armed citizens) were created. By 2016, the local forest was recovering and Cheran was the safest town in the area — no one had been murdered for a year. In comparison, the rest of the state of Michoacan had more than 180 murders in July 2016 alone.

2 Many powerful criminal gangs are based in Mexico, and as a result, the rule of law in the country has become weaker. The rule of law is an essential part of any democratic system and it consists of three parts. The first is that everyone is able to use lawyers and the law to try to find solutions to the problems they have. The second part is that the law must be impartial. This means that people can be confident that the police and the government will treat everybody in the same way, whether they are rich or poor. The final part is that the law must apply to everybody. This means that the law is the same for the poorest and weakest people in society as it is for the wealthiest and most powerful people. But how does this work in practice?

Themis, the Goddess of Justice, wears a blindfold so that she treats everybody fairly.

3 Hiring a lawyer and going to court can be expensive and take a lot of time. Naturally, this is easier for rich people than it is for poor people. Many countries provide free legal services for poor people, but these services are often overworked. For example, in the U.S. state of Florida in 2013, lawyers in the public service worked on more than 1,000 cases each. This meant that, on average, they spent less than one hour preparing for each case. One result of this is that the poor are more likely to go to prison than the rich. And money can be useful even in prison. For example, in 2016, police discovered that some prisoners in Topo Chico prison in northern Mexico were living in cells that had air-conditioning, saunas, refrigerators, televisions, luxury baths, and even aquariums. Perhaps it is no surprise that there is an English saying that, "there is one law for the rich, and another for the poor."

Money shouldn't be able to buy justice.

Chapter 17 I'll See You in Court! — *What Is the Rule of Law?*

51

4 Another famous proverb is that "the punishment must fit the crime." In other words, the more serious the crime, the more a criminal should be punished. Perhaps most people would agree with this idea, but what about capital punishment — should murderers pay for their crimes with their own lives? Today, less than one third of countries have a capital punishment law, and as few as 20 still use it. In 5 fact, most of the world's executions take place in just five countries: China, Iran, Pakistan, Saudi Arabia, and the United States. But why have so many countries given up capital punishment? The main reason is this: if the police and the courts make a mistake, it is easy to release someone from prison, but they cannot bring someone back to life. Since 1973, about 1,500 people have been executed in the United States. 10 Over the same time period, more than 150 people who were going to be executed were found to be innocent and released. No one knows how many innocent people have been executed. Is an error rate of at least 10 percent really acceptable? Most countries do not think so.

52

5 Even if we are confident that the police and the courts will treat us fairly, 15 what if the law itself is bad? This is the role of a country's supreme court. A supreme court ensures that the laws made by politicians are in line with the constitution of the country, and that politicians cannot use the law to increase their own power and wealth by taking the rights of the people away. For example, in 1954, the U.S. Supreme Court decided that it was wrong to teach white students and black 20 students separately in different schools, even though many politicians and many white Americans thought it was a good idea. It should be no surprise that the media often reports on conflicts between the government and the country's supreme court.

53

6 How important is the rule of law? Every year, the World Justice Project publishes a list ranking countries according to how strong their rule of law is. Those 25 countries where the rule of law is strongest — where people have confidence that they will be treated fairly, and that the courts and the police have the least interference from politicians — are also the countries where the people are the safest, freest, wealthiest, and happiest. In 2016, Japan was ranked 15th. We still have work to do.

NOTES ....

gangster「犯罪組織の一員」 **corrupt**「堕落した」 **town council**「町議会」 **murder** (v)「殺害する」 **the rule of law**「法の支配」 **impartial**「公平な」 **apply to ~**「~に適用される」 **in practice**「実際には」 **go to court**「裁判に訴える」 **cell**「(刑務所の) 監房」 **capital punishment**「極刑, 死刑」 **execution**「死刑執行」 **innocent**「無実の, 無罪の」

93

supreme court「最高裁判所」 in line with ~「〜と合致して」 conflict「対立」 **World Justice Project**「世界司法（正義）プロジェクト」世界で法の支配の促進活動を行う米国の非政府組織

Questions for Understanding

Part 1 *Look at the following statements. Write T if the statement is true, and F if it is false. Write the number of the paragraph where you find the answer in the parenthesis.*

1. One problem in the town of Cheran was that the police allowed some crimes to happen.

   T/F
   (#   )

2. The passage suggests that public service lawyers in Florida have too much work.

   T/F
   (#   )

3. The passage states that most people in the world agree with capital punishment.

   T/F
   (#   )

4. It is not unusual for a country's supreme court and the government to disagree.

   T/F
   (#   )

Part 2 *Look at the questions below. Check the best answer for each.*

1. Choose the word that has the closest meaning to "ensures" in the following sentence in Paragraph 5.

   A supreme court <u>ensures</u> that the laws made by politicians are in line with the constitution of the country, and that politicians cannot use the law to increase their own power and wealth by taking the rights of the people away.

   a. ☐ admits b. ☐ demonstrates c. ☐ guarantees d. ☐ notices

2. Which of the following is more likely for poor people than it is for rich people?

   a. ☐ Having a luxury bath b. ☐ Going to prison
   c. ☐ Joining a militia d. ☐ Hiring a lawyer and going to court

3. How many countries still execute some prisoners?

   a. ☐ 5 b. ☐ 10 c. ☐ 20 d. ☐ 150

4. What is not true about countries with a strong rule of law?

   a. ☐ They are safer. b. ☐ They have happier people.
   c. ☐ They have more crime. d. ☐ They are wealthier.

94

Chapter 17   **I'll See You in Court!** – *What Is the Rule of Law?*

Summary

② 54

Fill each space with the best word or phrase from the list below.

corrupt	rule of law	supreme	punished
innocent	(be) in line with		

Would you rather live in a country where the police always arrest criminals or one where a criminal can pay some money to a 1) _____ police officer and go free? In a democratic society, it is important that we are confident that 2) _____ people are not sent to prison and that criminals will be 3) _____ no matter how rich or important they are. The 4) _____, through the 5) _____ court, also ensures that the laws made by politicians 6) _____ the constitution of the country.

What do YOU think?

Choose ONE of the statements below. Do you agree or disagree with it? Why? Prepare a short response giving your opinion.

▶ Japan should stop using capital punishment.
▶ The punishment must fit the crime.

....

....

....

....

> *It seems to me that an unjust law is no law at all.*
>
> Augustine of Hippo (354-430)
> Christian theologian

95

Chapter 18

Just a Face in the Crowd?

What Does Equality Really Mean?

Useful Words

Choose a word or phrase from the list below to complete each sentence.

1. After a _____ of more than 300 years, women can now vote in every country.

2. She always does well in her tests, so she is _____ graduate at the top of her class.

3. I could not _____ a Business class ticket, so I bought an Economy class ticket instead.

4. I have straight blonde hair _____ my brother has curly brown hair.

5. It is difficult to _____ how long it will take to lose five kilograms of weight.

| while | struggle | likely to | afford | estimate |

Reading

② 55~61

55

1 Think, for a moment, about your friends. Perhaps there are differences in height, weight, hair color, sporting ability, or skill with games. Maybe some get high scores in some subjects, and do poorly in others. Some may have big families, while some may have very small ones. Even the places you have lived or your nationality
5 may be different. Do you believe that you and your friends are equal? The 1948 United Nations Universal Declaration of Human Rights begins by stating that "recognition of the inherent dignity and of the equal and inalienable rights of all members of the human family is the foundation of freedom, justice and peace in the world." But when people are so different from each other, what does it really mean
10 when we say that everybody is equal?

Chapter 18   **Just a Face in the Crowd?** – *What Does Equality Really Mean?*

2 We clearly live in an unequal world, and changing it may seem impossible. However, over the last 200 years huge changes have occurred that have made the world a more equal place. Today, democracy has spread to half of the world, slavery is a crime in every country, more than half of the countries in the world provide education to their citizens, and women have won the right to vote, work, and decide who they will marry. You may have grown up thinking that many of these things are "normal," but in fact, achieving these rights required hard work, struggle, and campaigning by previous generations.

Can you accept a world where some children have schools like this ...

... while others have schools like this?

3 Today, perhaps one of the greatest sources of inequality is income inequality. In 2013, a Gallup study reported that the global median annual income was about $3,000. The country with the highest annual median income was Norway, at $19,308, while the country with the lowest annual median income was the African nation of Zambia, at $287. There can also be huge differences within a single country. For example, median annual income in the United States was about $15,000. In 2016, Thomas M. Rutledge, the CEO of Charter Communications, earned $98 million. In other words, it took him only about three *hours* to earn the U.S. *annual* median income.

4 There is not only huge inequality in how much people earn, but also in who earns it. While half of all people are women, in 2017 only 6.4 percent of the CEOs of the world's top 500 companies were women. Furthermore, the participation of women in politics can be very low. In 2017, about 23 percent of politicians were women, and only two countries, Bolivia in South America and Rwanda in Africa, had governments which were more than 50 percent female. Fortunately, many countries have plans to increase the number of women involved in politics and running companies. For example, the Japanese government has a target of increasing the proportion of female executives and politicians to 30 percent. However, by 2017, fewer than 15 percent of Japanese politicians and only 3.4 percent of company executives were female.

5 It is easy to assume that inequality is the result of deliberate discrimination, that people are blocked from opportunities because of their gender, color, religion, or for some other reason. While this is a big problem, inequality can also arise without any real desire to discriminate. For example, if you live in an area where the price of a house is high, it is likely that poor people cannot afford to live there. Furthermore, the local taxes will be higher, which means that there will be cleaner streets, nicer parks, sports arenas, better schools, and so on. As a result, children growing up in that area will have many opportunities that children living in a poorer area will not. These wealthier children are then more likely to do well at school, go to university, get a better job, and to live in a wealthier area themselves. This will seem to be the normal way of life to them, and they may find it difficult to understand the lives of people who are less fortunate than themselves. Some of them may even begin to believe that they are special while poor people are lazy and stupid. Consequently inequality can continue from generation to generation.

6 Inequality has huge negative effects on society. The OECD estimates that gender inequality costs the global economy nearly $12 trillion a year. Inequality can even affect the length of your life. For example, in the United States, the average life expectancy of white people is 79.1 years, but for black people it is 75.5 years. In other words, if we want our countries to be wealthier and healthier, we must try to end inequality.

7 Inequality can only exist if we do nothing. If each of us takes some small action to reduce inequality, then big changes can occur. Some people may fear that equality will mean that everybody will be the same, but that is not what true equality is. Just as you treat your friends equally even though they are all different, true equality means that each person has the freedom and opportunities they need to become the best person that they can be. Will you continue the work of past generations? Will you help to create a future free of inequality?

NOTES ··

A Face in the Crowd 『群衆の中のひとつの顔』米国の映画。1957 年製作、エリア・カザン監督が手がけた社会派ドラマ。　**the United Nations Universal Declaration of Human Rights** ※ Chapter 16 を参照　**inherent dignity**「固有の尊厳」　**inalienable right**「譲ることのできない権利」　**slavery**「奴隷制」　**campaigning**「(ある目的を達成するための) 運動・働き掛け」　**Gallup**「ギャラップ」米国の世論調査会社　**median**「中央値」資料の全てを大きさの順に並べたときに、中央にくる数値　**CEO** (= chief executive officer)「最高経営責任

Chapter 18　**Just a Face in the Crowd?** – *What Does Equality Really Mean?*

者」　**Charter Communications**「チャーター・コミュニケーションズ」米国のケーブルテレビ会社　**discrimination**「差別」　**gender**「性（別）」　**OECD** ※ Chapter 4 を参照　**life expectancy**「平均余命」

Questions for Understanding

Part 1　*Look at the following statements. Write T if the statement is true, and F if it is false. Write the number of the paragraph where you find the answer in the parenthesis.*

1. The Universal Declaration of Human Rights tells us that we all have the same rights.

　T/F
　(#　　)

2. Inequality can exist not only between people but also between countries.

　T/F
　(#　　)

3. The passage informs us that inequality in a society can sometimes develop unintentionally.

　T/F
　(#　　)

4. According to the passage, there is no way to end inequality because we are all different.

　T/F
　(#　　)

Part 2　*Look at the questions below. Check the best answer for each.*

1. According to the passage, what is true equality?
   a. ☐ Making sure everyone can achieve their potential.
   b. ☐ Making sure that global median income rises.
   c. ☐ Making sure that half of CEOs and politicians are women.
   d. ☐ Making sure that black people and white people are treated the same.

2. How long did it take Thomas M. Rutledge to earn the global annual median income?
   a. ☐ About 30 minutes　　　b. ☐ About 3 hours
   c. ☐ About 3 days　　　　　d. ☐ About 1 year

3. In Japan, what percentage of company executives are male?
   a. ☐ 3.4%　　b. ☐ 6.4%　　c. ☐ 23%　　d. ☐ 96.6%

4. Choose the word that has the closest meaning to "deliberate" in the following sentence in Paragraph 5.
   It is easy to assume that inequality is the result of <u>deliberate</u> discrimination, that people are blocked from opportunities because of their gender, color, religion, or for some other reason.
   a. ☐ intentional　　b. ☐ serious　　c. ☐ thoughtful　　d. ☐ unnecessary

99

Summary

② 62

Fill each space with the best word from the list below.

| affects | fortunate | median | discrimination | inherent | deliberate |

The 1) _____ rights we have today are the result of the suffering and struggles of past generations. However, while we are 2) _____ to live in the modern world, the fight to end inequality is not over. Today, many forms of 3) _____ still exist, such as gender and wealth inequality. Even in the richest countries, the 4) _____ income of men and women are quite different. In the past this inequality was the result of a 5) _____ decision to pay women less than men, but today it is because there are still too few women in the most highly paid jobs. Inequality 6) _____ us all, and so we all have a responsibility to continue the fight against it.

What do YOU think?

Choose ONE of the statements below. Do you agree or disagree with it? Why? Prepare a short response giving your opinion.

▶ Inequality is not a problem because it encourages people to change their lives.
▶ Reducing inequality among countries will result in a more peaceful world.

> *We may have democracy, or we may have wealth concentrated in the hands of a few, but we can't have both.*
>
> Louis Brandeis (1856-1941)
> U.S. Supreme Court Justice (1916-39)

Chapter 19
Freedom of the Press Means Freedom of the People
The Danger of Fake News

Useful Words

Choose a word or phrase from the list below to complete each sentence.

1. The Internet _____ us to obtain information about almost anything at any time.

2. The _____ of an election cannot be known until all the votes have been counted.

3. Unfortunately, _____ are a common occurrence in the United States.

4. The company president was _____ for the terrible results.

5. The _____ of cars has improved over the last 50 years and they rarely break down today.

| blamed | mass shootings | reliability | allows | outcome |

Reading

1 The number of people connected to the Internet is now over 3 billion. The easy availability of websites, e-mail, and social media means that anyone can create and share their own content, such as pictures, videos, and stories. As a result, at any given time, hundreds of millions of people are reading, watching, liking, writing, sharing,

Mark Zuckerberg, the CEO of Facebook, has admitted that fake news may have affected major events. Facebook is the largest platform in the world for social media.

and chatting about online content. However, while Internet freedom and access is a good thing, it also allows those with more sinister motives to spread information which is exaggerated, distorted, or simply made up. This kind of content is often called fake news. Fake news is an important issue because it can influence the
5 behavior of such large groups of people particularly if it is driven by organizations and individuals skilled in exploiting the various technologies available. In 2018, for example, Mark Zuckerberg, the founder of Facebook, admitted that fake news posted on Facebook could have affected the outcome of the 2016 U.S. presidential election.

64

10 **2** Some fake news is satire or parody. *The Onion* is one good example of this. It is clear to visitors to the site that the stories are fiction, but they highlight an important social issue through humorous (and fake) articles that illustrate an important point. For example, after the February 2018 shooting at Stoneman Douglas High School in Florida, *The Onion* used the headline, "Idea Of Doing Nothing Until Next Mass
15 Shooting Quickly Gaining Traction In Congress," to indicate the frustration many people felt at how little the U.S. government had done to prevent such tragedies.

65

3 However, while the aim of satire is to make us laugh, and then to think about how we can make our societies better, most fake news has very different goals. Freedom House, a U.S. non-governmental organization that aims to increase freedom
20 and democracy around the world, has identified more than 30 governments that pay people to spread ideas that support the government. For example, a "keyboard army" was used to operate fake Facebook accounts and to support Rodrigo Duterte during the 2016 presidential election in the Philippines. In a 2017 report, Freedom House concluded that such online manipulation and misinformation had affected
25 the results of 18 elections around the world during 2016.

66

4 Fake news can also be used to spread negative ideas, stereotypes, and conspiracies about different countries, races, and genders. For example, after the Sutherland Springs church shooting in Texas in 2017 that left 26 people dead, a picture of U.S. comedian Sam Hyde was posted online falsely claiming that he was the
30 gunman. The people who did this also blamed Sam Hyde for the 2015 Paris attacks, the 2015 San Bernardino shooting, the 2016 Orlando nightclub shooting, and the 2017 Las Vegas shooting. In 2018, the Japanese embassy in Washington, D.C. had to make a public statement because of a popular piece of fake news claiming that a

restaurant in Japan sold human meat, and that the Japanese government had made cannibalism legal.

5 Fake news can be dangerous and even deadly. In the month before the 2016 U.S. presidential election, fake news websites received 159 million visits. One of the fake news stories claimed that some politicians were involved in illegal sexual activities with children in a pizza restaurant called Comet Ping Pong in Washington, D.C. As a result, hundreds of people threatened the staff of the restaurant, and on December 4, 2016, a man fired a gun inside the restaurant. Fortunately, nobody was hurt. The next day, a new fake news story claimed the attack was a fake. Another illustration of the danger of fake news relates to vaccines being dangerous. Even though there is no scientific evidence for such beliefs, these ideas have been spread online for more than 20 years. As a result, some worried parents have not vaccinated their children, and hundreds are said to have died unnecessary deaths.

6 Fake news spreads so easily because most of us do not think carefully about news stories or check their reliability. Fake news spreads because a well-written lie with a simple message can be easy to believe, while the truth is often difficult and complex. How can we spot fake news? First, we should check to see if the same story is being shared by many trustworthy news sites. We should check to see if there is any evidence that supports the claim in the story. We should consider what it would mean if the story was true, and how that matches with the world we know. Finally, we should be suspicious of stories that promise a simple answer to a difficult problem.

7 One of the reasons that so many democracies protect the right to free speech and, consequently the freedom of the press, is that people need to be well-informed in order to choose their politicians wisely. Fake news makes that harder. If we do not learn how to identify and stop fake news, we allow it to encourage hatred, threaten our health, put our lives in danger, and weaken our democracy. In the fight against lies and liars we must all speak the truth more loudly.

It is advisable to get news from trusted sources, but fake news is getting harder to identify.

NOTES

freedom of the press「報道・出版・言論の自由」　**social media**「ソーシャルメディア」インターネット上で個人が情報を発信・交換・共有することで形成される情報交流サービスの総称。具体的にはブログ、電子掲示板、SNS（ソーシャル・ネットワーキング・サービス）、画像や動画の投稿共有サイトなど。情報を一方的に発信する従来型のマスメディア（新聞やテレビなど）とは異なり、不特定多数または特定のメンバーでやりとりを行う双方向メディアである。代表的なものはツイッター、フェイスブック、ユーチューブなど。　**content**「コンテンツ」テレビやインターネットで伝達される、教養や娯楽のために創造または編集された情報内容。映画、音楽、アニメ作品、ゲーム、小説など。　**at any given time**「いつでも」　**sinister motive**「悪意のある動機」　**exaggerated**「誇張された」　**distorted**「ゆがめられた；曲解された」　**exploit**「悪用する」　**satire**「風刺，皮肉」　***The Onion***『オニオン紙』ウェブ上で発行する米国の風刺新聞。　**gain traction**「勢いづく」　**tragedy**「惨事」　**non-governmental organization** (= NGO)「非政府組織」　**Rodrigo Duterte**「ロドリゴ・ドゥテルテ」フィリピンの大統領。2016 年 6 月 30 日就任（任期 6 年）。**manipulation**「操作，改ざん」　**stereotype**「ステレオタイプ」ある集団で共通に受け入れられている単純化、固定化された概念やイメージ。単純化でゆがめられたイメージとなる場合があり、偏見や差別につながる危険性がある。　**conspiracy**「陰謀」　**2015 Paris attacks** ※ Chapter 9 を参照　**2015 San Bernardino shooting** 2015 年 12 月 2 日に米カリフォルニア州サンバーナディーノの福祉施設で起きた銃乱射事件。14 人が死亡。　**2016 Orlando nightclub shooting** 2016 年 6 月 12 日未明に米フロリダ州オーランドのナイトクラブ起きた銃乱射事件。49 人が死亡。**2017 Las Vegas shooting** 2017 年 10 月 1 日夜に米ネバダ州ラスベガスでコンサート会場を狙った米史上最悪の銃乱射事件。58 人が死亡。　**cannibalism**「人肉食」　**vaccinate**「ワクチンによる予防接種をする」

Questions for Understanding

Part 1　*Look at the following statements. Write T if the statement is true, and F if it is false. Write the number of the paragraph where you find the answer in the parenthesis.*

1. Fake news can have a big impact on behavior and large events.

   T/F
   (#　　　)

2. *The Onion* helped to prevent a mass shooting in Florida.

   T/F
   (#　　　)

3. Most governments employ a "keyboard army" to deliver the message they want.

   T/F
   (#　　　)

4. The pizza restaurant Comet Ping Pong was a real crime scene.

   T/F
   (#　　　)

104

Chapter 19 **Freedom of the Press Means Freedom of the People** — *The Danger of Fake News*

Part 2   *Look at the questions below. Check the best answer for each.*

1. Which of the following cannot be clearly associated with fake news?
    a. ☐ Distorting a news story   b. ☐ Sharing a news story
    c. ☐ Exaggerating a news story   d. ☐ Making up a news story

2. What is the aim of the Freedom House organization?
    a. ☐ To identify fake news
    b. ☐ To advise governments how to handle the Internet and social media
    c. ☐ To protect and preserve democracy and freedom
    d. ☐ To identify "keyboard armies" and stop them

3. Why is Sam Hyde well-known on the Internet?
    a. ☐ He is regularly falsely blamed for various crimes.
    b. ☐ He is a popular comedian.
    c. ☐ He carried out several shootings between 2015 and 2017.
    d. ☐ He sold human meat to a restaurant.

4. What are three ways to spot fake news?
    a. ☐ Check sources, find the story in more than one place, and check
       popular stories on social media.
    b. ☐ Look for trustworthy news sites, check sources, and be suspicious.
    c. ☐ Identify true stories, make comments online, and confirm the truth by
       making comments on social media.
    d. ☐ Look for evidence, look for good quality writing, and write a blog
       post about it.

105

Summary

Fill each space with the best word from the list below.

| identify | distort | exploit | trustworthy | availability | sinister |

The 1) _____ of so much information online means we have to be careful about what we believe. While many sources are 2) _____, others have more 3) _____ motives and may seek to exaggerate, 4) _____, or make up news items. This can be particularly powerful if the creator of this fake news is able to 5) _____ social media to spread the message to large numbers of people. Fake news can influence opinion and change behavior so it is a very important issue. There are a number of ways we can try to 6) _____ fake news, such as using well-known news sites and checking sources. It is also important to be somewhat suspicious of everything we read online.

What do YOU think?

Choose ONE of the statements below. Do you agree or disagree with it? Why? Prepare a short response giving your opinion.

▶ Fake news is useful if you want to try to influence an event or people's opinions.
▶ The only thing that matters is the truth — the discovery of this should be everyone's objective.

A lie can travel half way around the world while the truth is putting on its shoes.

Mark Twain (1835-1910)
American author

Chapter 20 One in a Million

Why *Your* Vote Counts

Useful Words

Choose a word from the list below to complete each sentence.

1. Before you leave tonight, please _____ that you turn out the lights and lock the door.

2. Jō was chosen to be the _____ for our class on the student council.

3. All of the hours you study will not _____ if you do not pass the test.

4. His plan to drive around Europe in the summer was _____ — he could not drive.

5. Yumi gave the final _____ to the graduating class at the graduation ceremony.

flawed	count	ensure	address	representative

Reading

② 71~78

71

1 Since 2006, the Economist Intelligence Unit, a British research company, has published the Democracy Index, which examines how democratic different countries are. According to the 2017 report, 49.3 percent of the world's population live in a democratic country, the highest ever result. So why has democracy been described as "the worst form of government except all those other forms that have 5 been tried"?

72

2 One problem is that only 4.5 percent of people live in countries that are full democracies. In those countries, the rule of law is strong, the media are free and

107

independent, and human rights are encouraged and protected. Furthermore, elections are free, fair, and most people take part. However, many people live in countries which are flawed democracies, where there are problems with one or more aspects of democracy. You may be surprised to learn that not only are the United States of America and Japan considered to be flawed democracies, but also that the reason is the same: low participation.

Can you think of a better way to choose your government?

73

3 In the 2016 U.S. presidential election, 55.7 percent of voters cast a vote. In the 2014 Lower House election in Japan, 52 percent of voters cast a vote. Compare this to recent elections in countries like Australia, Belgium, Denmark, Iceland, Norway, South Korea, and Sweden where more than 75 percent of voters cast a vote. Why is low participation a problem?

74

4 In 1863, U.S. president Abraham Lincoln gave his most famous speech, the Gettysburg Address. In it, he tells us that democracy is "government of the people, by the people, for the people." However, if only about half of voters take part in an election, then the government is being chosen by one quarter of the voters. In other words, three quarters of voters *did not vote* for the government. Is this "government of the people, by the people, for the people"? Furthermore, low voter participation means that it is easier for politicians to be influenced by special interest groups. For example, the National Rifle Association (NRA), a U.S. organization created to protect the right of American citizens to bear arms, has 5 million members. The NRA donates a lot of money to politicians who support the ownership of guns, and encourages NRA members to vote for such politicians. As a result, for many years the NRA has been able to prevent laws that control or limit the ownership of guns in the United States. It is difficult to say if most Americans agree with the ideas of the NRA, but it is clear that the 5 million NRA members have a disproportionate amount of political power.

75

5 Abraham Lincoln's words do not only tell us what democracy is, they also remind us that we are responsible for our governments because we choose our politicians. If you do not vote in an election, you have lost your opportunity to show what kind of government and political ideas you support. In addition, if you do not vote, then politicians have no reason to listen to you. If you are happy with your political representatives, you should vote to support them. If you are not happy with your political representatives, you should vote to change them. Having a vote means that you share the responsibility to make your society better. As Martin Luther King III said, "If we are to be a great democracy, we must all take an active role in our democracy. We must do democracy. That goes far beyond simply casting your vote. We must all actively champion the causes that ensure the common good."

Will you take part in the next election?

6 Furthermore, while one vote cast among millions may seem to be insignificant, it is not. Every vote is as important as the rest, and every vote counts. In a local election in the U.S. state of Virginia in 2017, David Yancey received 11,607 votes. His opponent, Shelley Simonds, received 11,608 votes. When the votes were recounted, both were found to have 11,608 votes. Yancey finally won the election after a random draw. Similarly close election results have been recorded in many other democratic countries.

7 However, if none of the politicians seem to care about the same things that you do, then maybe you should stand for election and vote for yourself. After all, as former U.S. president Barack Obama said, "Our democracy is not the buildings, not the monuments. It's you being willing to work to make things better and being willing to listen to each other and argue with each other and come together and knock on doors and make phone calls and treat people with respect."

8 Democracy is not perfect. Our politicians often disappoint us, and taking part in the political process can seem to be pointless. But it is not. In a democracy we are able to choose our government and more importantly, every few years we can assess its performance and change it. Your vote is a responsibility, a duty, and a hard-won right. Use it, and use it well, because in countries without democracy the only way to change the government is through violence and war.

NOTES

Economist Intelligence Unit「エコノミスト・インテリジェンス・ユニット」英経済誌『エコノミスト』の調査部門　**Democracy Index**「民主主義指数」各国・地域の民主主義の水準を測る指数。選挙手続きと多元主義、市民の自由、政府の機能、政治への参加、政治文化の5つの部門から評価している。　**Democracy is the worst form of government except all those other forms that have been tried.**「民主主義は、これまでに試みられた他の全ての政治形態を除けば、最悪の形態である」　**full democracy**「完全な民主主義国」　**rule of law**「法の支配」　**media**「（マス）メディア」新聞、ラジオ、テレビなどのマスコミュニケーションの媒体。media は medium の複数形で、通常は複数形で使用される。　**flawed democracy**「欠陥のある民主主義国」　**Lower House**「衆議院」　**Gettysburg Address**「ゲティズバーグ演説」米国第16代大統領のリンカーンがペンシルベニア州ゲティズバーグで行った演説。　**special interest group**「特定利益団体」　**National Rifle Association (NRA)**「全米ライフル協会（NRA）」　**bear arms**「武器を所持する」　**donate**「寄付する」　**disproportionate**「（程度などが）不均衡な」　**Martin Luther King III**「マーティン・ルーサー・キング3世（1957-）」米国の人権活動家。20世紀半ばに公民権運動を主導した故マーティン・ルーサー・キング・ジュニア（Martin Luther King Jr.：1929-68）牧師の長男。　**cause**「大義，理念」　**common good**「公益」　**insignificant**「わずかな，重要でない」　**stand for election**「選挙に立候補する」　**pointless**「無意味な」　**assess**「評価する」　**hard-won**「苦労して獲得した」

◢ Questions for Understanding

Part 1　*Look at the following statements. Write T if the statement is true, and F if it is false. Write the number of the paragraph where you find the answer in the parenthesis.*

1. According to the passage, most forms of government are better than democracy.

   T/F
   (#　　　)

2. The government will not know what we think if we do not vote.

   T/F
   (#　　　)

3. In a democracy, a single person's vote has little value.

   T/F
   (#　　　)

4. Because we can change the government by voting, we should vote in every election.

   T/F
   (#　　　)

Chapter 20   **One in a Million** – *Why Your Vote Counts*

Part 2 *Look at the questions below. Check the best answer for each.*

1. Which of the following is correct?
   a. ☐ Nearly half of the countries in the world are democracies.
   b. ☐ More than half of the countries in the world are democracies.
   c. ☐ Nearly half of the people in the world live in a democracy.
   d. ☐ More than half of the people in the world live in a democracy.

2. From highest to lowest, which is the correct order of voter participation?
   a. ☐ Japan, USA, Australia
   b. ☐ Iceland, USA, Japan
   c. ☐ South Korea, Japan, USA
   d. ☐ USA, Denmark, Japan

3. What is the NRA?
   a. ☐ It is a group that tries to influence political decisions.
   b. ☐ It is a company that sells guns.
   c. ☐ It is an U.S. political party.
   d. ☐ It is an organization that collect money for election campaigns.

4. Choose the word or phrase that has the closest meaning to "champion" in the following sentence in Paragraph 5.
   We must all actively <u>champion</u> the causes that ensure the common good.
   a. ☐ adopt
   b. ☐ interfere with
   c. ☐ oppose
   d. ☐ stand up for

111

Summary

Fill each space with the best word or phrase from the list below.

> pointless   opponent   disproportionate   champion   insignificant
> rule of law

Why should you vote? One vote among millions seems 1)_____. Surely voting is a/an 2)_____ activity in a safe and wealthy country like Japan. However, to win an election a politician needs only one vote more than their 3)_____ receives. Furthermore, the number of votes each politician receives allows them to assess the popularity of their policies. If you do not vote, who will 4)_____ you in government? If you do not vote, how will you ensure that politicians follow the 5)_____? If you do not vote, you give the people that DO vote 6)_____ power — power over your life. Why should you vote? Because it is your right, your duty, your responsibility, and your life.

What do YOU think?

Choose ONE of the statements below. Do you agree or disagree with it? Why? Prepare a short response giving your opinion.

> ▶ Everybody should be required to vote in an election.
> ▶ It would be better if some people were not allowed to vote.

> *Bad officials are elected by good citizens who do not vote.*
>
> George Jean Nathan (1882-1958)
> American author

Compiled References by Chapter

Many references were consulted in writing this book. The following is a list of the most useful, and we direct students and teachers who are interested in learning more about the issues raised in this book to them.

Chapter 1   Building Blocks, Building Minds – The Amazing Success of Lego

- Antorini, Y. M., Muñiz., A. M., Askildsen, T. (2012). Collaborating with customer communities: Lessons from the Lego Group, *MIT Sloan Management Review, 53*(3), pp.73-95.
- Antorini, Y. M., Muñiz., A. M. (2013). The benefits and challenges of collaborating with user communities, *Research-Technology Management, 56*(3), pp.21-28.
- BBC News (2018)."Lego goes green with sugarcane-based plastic," BBC News, 2 March 2018, <https://www.bbc.com/news/business-43253798>.
- BBC News (2018). "Lego: The invention of the legendary brick," BBC News, 27 Jan 2018, <https://www.bbc.com/news/av/stories-42821594/lego-the-invention-of-the-legendary-brick>
- "Brickfilm," *Wikipedia.org*, <https://en.wikipedia.org/wiki/Brickfilm>.
- The Brickfan, <https://www.thebrickfan.com/>.
- Brosnan, M. J. (1998). Spatial Ability in Children's Play with Lego Blocks, *Perceptual and Motor Skills, 87*(1), pp.19-28.
- Cuusoo.com, <http://lego.cuusoo.com>.
- "*FIRST* LEGO League," *Wikipedia.org*, <https://en.wikipedia.org/wiki/FIRST_Lego_League>.
- Kristiansen, P. & Rasmussen, R. (2014). *Building a Better Business Using the Lego Serious Play Method*, John Wiley & Sons, Hoboken
- "Lego Mindstorms," *Wikipedia.org*, <https://en.wikipedia.org/wiki/Lego_Mindstorms>.
- "The Lego Movie," *Wikipedia.org*, <https://en.wikipedia.org/wiki/The_Lego_Movie>.
- "Lego Studios," *Wikipedia.org*, <https://en.wikipedia.org/wiki/Lego_Studios>.
- Legoff, D. B., Sherman, M. (2006). Long-term outcome of social skills intervention based on interactive LEGO© play, *Autism, 10*(4), pp.317-329.
- "Legoland," *Wikipedia.org*, <https://en.wikipedia.org/wiki/Legoland>
- Milne, R.(2017). "Lego suffers first drop in revenues in a decade," *The Financial Times*, 5 September 2017, <https://www.ft.com/content/d5e0b6b0-9211-11e7-a9e6-11d2f0ebb7f0>.
- Lego.com, (2017). "New App Brings Lego Bricks to Life,"*Lego.com, 5 December 2017,* <https://www.lego.com/en-us/aboutus/news-room/2017/december/lego-ar-studio/>
- Sharifi Asl E. & Asadin, S. (2016). Lego: A tool to improve problem solving and teamwork skills of students in science, *Journal of Technology and Education, 10*(2), pp.133-144.
- Reuters (2017). "Toymaker Lego wins Chinese copyright case against brick imitators," *Reuters*, 7 December 2017, <https://www.reuters.com/article/us-lego-china-copyright/toymaker-lego-wins-chinese-copyright-case-against-brick-imitators-idUSKBN1E1157>.
- Lego Club TV, (2012). "The Lego Story,"*YouTube.com,* 10 Aug 2012, <https://www.youtube.com/watch?v=NdDU_BBJW9Y>.
- Wolfgang, C., Stannard, L. & Jones, I. (2010). Advanced constructional play with LEGOs among preschoolers as a predictor of later school achievement in mathematics, *Early Child Development and Care, 173*(5), pp.467-475.
- "World Robot Olympiad," *Wikipedia.org*, <https://en.wikipedia.org/wiki/World_Robot_Olympiad>.

Chapter 2   Faster, Higher, Stronger – The World's Most Extreme Sports

- 4 Deserts <http://www.4deserts.com/>.
- "2016 Summer Olympics," *Wikipedia.org*, <https://en.wikipedia.org/wiki/2016_Summer_Olympics>.
- BBC News. (2017). "How the UK Wife Carrying winners pulled off their win," BBC News, 6 March 2017, <http://www.bbc.com/news/uk-39176901>.
- Chia, A. (2017). Indoor skydiving: Singaporean teen Kyra Poh wins two golds at Wind Games in Spain, *The Strait Times*, 5 February 2017, <http://www.straitstimes.com/sport/indoor-skydiving-singaporean-teen-kyra-poh-wins-two-golds-at-wind-games-in-spain>.
- International Wife Carrying Competition, <http://eukonkanto.fi/>.

- Ironman, <http://ap.ironman.com/#axzz4bYsqSgFd>.
- "Ironman Triathlon," *Wikipedia.org*, <https://en.wikipedia.org/wiki/Ironman_Triathlon>.
- Scott, R., Cayla, J., Cova, B. (2017). Selling Pain to the Saturated Self, *Journal of Consumer Research*, ucw071. doi: 10.1093/jcr/ucw071
- "Serge Girard," *Wikipedia.org*, <https://en.wikipedia.org/wiki/Serge_Girard>.
- "Tough Mudder," *Wikipedia.org*, <https://en.wikipedia.org/wiki/Tough_Mudder>.

Chapter 3   Do You Hulu? – The Future of Television

- The Economist (2016). "The future of television – Cutting the cord," *The Economist*,16 June 2016, < https://www.economist.com/news/business/21702177-television-last-having-its-digital-revolution-moment-cutting-cord>.
- "Netflix," *Wikipedia.org*, <https://en.wikipedia.org/wiki/Netflix>.
- Ovide, S., (2018). "Netflix's Growth Is in the Eye of the Beholder", *Bloomberg.com*, 22 January 2018, <https://www.bloomberg.com/amp/gadfly/articles/2018-01-22/netflix-earnings-growth-is-in-the-eye-of-the-beholder>.
- Statista <www.statista.com>.
- Sweney, M.,(2018). "BT chief: We don't need Premier League rights," 2 February 2018, *The Guardian*, <https://www.theguardian.com/media/2018/feb/02/bt-chief-we-dont-need-premier-league-rights>.
- Williams, C., (2015). "The future of TV, as Sky sees it – virtual reality and beyond," 3 Oct 2015, *The Telegraph*, <https://www.telegraph.co.uk/finance/newsbysector/mediatechnologyandtelecoms/11909310/The-future-of-TV-as-Sky-sees-it-virtual-reality-and-beyond.html>.
- Williams, R., (2015). "Apple TV: The history of Apple's bid to take over your living room,"8 September 2015, *The Telegraph*, <https://www.telegraph.co.uk/technology/apple/11849521/Apple-TV-The-story-of-Apples-bid-to-take-over-your-living-room.html>.

Chapter 4   A Woman's Place is ~~in the Kitchen~~ Wherever She Wants – Gender Equality

- "1975 Icelandic Women's Strike," *Wikipedia.org*, <https://en.wikipedia.org/wiki/1975_Icelandic_women's_strike>.
- Ferrant, G. & Nowacka, K. (2015). Measuring the drivers of gender inequality and their impact on development: the role of discriminatory social institutions, *Gender and Development, 23*(2), pp.319-332.
- Ferrant, G. (2015). How Do Gender Inequalities Hinder Development? Cross-Country Evidence, *Annals of Economics and Statistics, 117-118*, pp.313-352.
- Ferrant, G. & Kolev, A. (2016). *The economic cost of gender-based discrimination in social institutions*, OECD Development Centre: Paris.
- Goldin, C. & Katz, L. (2002). The Power of the Pill: Oral Contraceptives and Women's Career and Marriage Decisions. *Journal of Political Economy. 110*(4), pp.730-770.
- Grabowska, A. (2017). Sex on the brain: Are gender‐dependent structural and functional differences associated with behavior?, *Journal of Neuroscience Research*, *95*(1-2), pp.200-212.
- Heron, M. (2016). Deaths: Leading Causes for 2014, *National Vital Statistics Reports, 65*(5), pp.1-96.
- "Hiromi Miyake," *Wikipedia.org*, <https://en.wikipedia.org/wiki/Hiromi_Miyake>.
- Hyde, J. S. (2016). Sex and cognition: gender and cognitive functions, *Current opinion in neurobiology, 38*, pp.53-56.
- Paley, V. (1984). *Boys and Girls: Superheroes in the Doll Corner*, University of Chicago Press: Chicago.
- *The State of Women-Owned Businesses, 2016*. American Express Open, 2016.
- *Integrated Postsecondary Education Data System (IPEDS), Fall 2016, Completions component*. U.S. Department of Education, National Center for Education Statistics, 2016.
- "The World's Highest Paid Actors, 2016", *Forbes*, <https://www.forbes.com/actors/#6477cda840fe>.
- Steele, J. R., Nalini, A. (2006). "Math is Hard!" The effect of gender priming on women's attitudes, *Journal of Experimental Social Psychology, 42*(4), pp.428-436.
- UNICEF (2013). *Ending Child Marriage: Progress and prospects*, United Nations International Children's Emergency Fund: New York.

Chapter 5   The Internet of Things – This Changes Everything

- Ferber, S., (2013) "How the Internet of Things Changes Everything," 7 May 2013, *The Harvard Business Review*, <https://hbr.org/2013/05/how-the-internet-of-things-cha>.
- Meola, A., (2016). "Internet of Things devices, applications & examples," 19 Dec 2016, *Business Insider*, <http://www.businessinsider.com/internet-of-things-devices-applications-examples-2016-8>.
- Morgan, J., (2014), "A Simple Explanation Of 'The Internet Of Things'," 13 May 2014, *Forbes*, <https://www.forbes.com/sites/jacobmorgan/2014/05/13/simple-explanation-internet-things-that-anyone-can-understand/#6239d3221d09>.
- Nest, <https://nest.com/uk/>.
- Phillips Hue, <https://www.philips.co.uk/c-m-li/hue>
- The Telegraph, "10 technologies that will make the Internet of Things a reality," *The Telegraph*, <https://www.telegraph.co.uk/technology/ces/11340738/10-technologies-that-will-make-the-Internet-of-Things-a-reality.html>.
- World Economic Forum, (2017). "Digital Transformation Initiative – In collaboration with Accenture – Unlocking $100 Trillion for Business and Society from Digital Transformation Executive Summary," *World Economic Forum*, <https://www.accenture.com/t20170116T084450__w__/us-en/_acnmedia/Accenture/Conversion-Assets/WEF/PDF/Accenture-DTI-executive-summary.pdf>.

Chapter 6   The Supercomputer in Your Pocket – How Cell Phones Have Changed the World

- "CDC 6600," *Wikipedia.org*, <https://en.wikipedia.org/wiki/CDC_6600>.
- "The Control Data Corporation," *Cray-Cyber.org*, <http://www.cray-cyber.org/memory/cdc.php>.
- Cowley, S. (2017). Banks Look to Cellphones to Replace A.T.M. Cards, *The New York Times*, 13 February 2017, <http://www.frbsf.org/cash/publications/fed-notes/2016/november/state-of-cash-2015-diary-consumer-payment-choice>.
- Demarest, E. & Ludwig, H. (2016). Armed man live-Tweeted police chase, prosecutors say, *dainfo.com*, 8 August 2016, <https://www.dnainfo.com/chicago/20160808/beverly/armed-man-live-tweeted-police-chase-prosecutors-say>.
- "IPhone 6," *Wikipedia.org*, <https://en.wikipedia.org/wiki/IPhone_6>.
- Kessler, G. (2013). Smartphones help catch a terror suspect, *cnn.com*, 24 April 2013, <http://edition.cnn.com/2013/04/24/opinion/kessler-digital-forensics>.
- Knysna-Plett Herald. (2014). "Smartphone leads to arrest of groper," *Knysna-Plett Herald*, 5 June 2014, <http://www.knysnaplettherald.com/news/News/International/77773/smartphone-leads-to-arrest-of-groper-20170711>.
- "M-Pesa," *Vodafone.com*, <http://www.vodafone.com/content/index/what/m-pesa.html>.
- "M-Pesa," *Wikipedia.org*, <https://en.wikipedia.org/wiki/M-Pesa>.
- "Processing Power Compared," *Experts Exchange.com*, <http://pages.experts-exchange.com/processing-power-compared/>.
- Rice, D. & Filippelli, G. (2010). One cell phone at a time: Countering corruption in Afghanistan, *Small Wars Journal*, September 2010, <http://smallwarsjournal.com/jrnl/art/one-cell-phone-at-a-time-countering-corruption-in-afghanistan>.
- Searcey, D. & Barry, J. Y. (2016). Inspired by the U.S., West Africans Wield Smartphones to Fight Police Abuse, *The New York Times*, 16 September 2016, <https://www.nytimes.com/2016/09/17/world/africa/police-abuse-videos-west-africa.html?mcubz=0>.
- "防犯アプリ Digi Police," *Tokyo Metropolitan Police*, <http://www.keishicho.metro.tokyo.jp/kurashi/tokushu/furikome/digipolice.html>.

Chapter 7   Land, Sea, and Air – How Drones Are Changing Our Lives

- "2015 Tokyo Drone Incident," *Wikipedia.org*, <https://en.wikipedia.org/wiki/2015_Tokyo_Drone_Incident>.
- Dinan, S. (2017). "Drones become latest tool drug cartels use to smuggle drugs into U.S.," *The Washington Times*, 20 August 2017, <https://www.washingtontimes.com/news/2017/aug/20/mexican-drug-cartels-using-drones-to-smuggle-heroi/>.
- "Drone Racing," *Wikipedia.org*, <https://en.wikipedia.org/wiki/Drone_racing>.
- "Drone Racing League," *Wikipedia.org*, <https://en.wikipedia.org/wiki/Drone_Racing_League>.
- Eku Online, "5 Ways Drones are Being Used for Disaster Relief," *ekuonline.com*, <https://safetymanagement.eku.edu/resources/articles/5-ways-drones-are-being-used-for-disaster-

relief/>.

- Etherington, D., "Drone Comes to the Rescue of Two Swimmers in Australia," *techcrunch.com*, 18 January 2018, <https://techcrunch.com/2018/01/18/drone-comes-to-the-rescue-of-two-swimmers-in-australia>.
- Hambling, D., (2018). Swarm of Drones Attack Airbase, 20 January 2018, *The New Scientist,* p12.
- "Holy Stone HS170 Predator Mini RC Helicopter Drone," *Amazon.com*, <https://www.amazon.com/Holy-Stone-Predator-Helicopter-Quadcopter/dp/B0157IHJMQ/ref=sr_1_5?s=toys-and-games&ie=UTF8&qid=1520821581&sr=1-5&keywords=drone&dpID=41fEnrMNvbL&preST=_SX300_QL70_&dpSrc=srch>.
- Jackson, T., (2017) "The flying drones that can scan packages night and day," BBC News, 27 October 2017, <http://www.bbc.com/news/business-41737300>.
- Joshi, D., (2017). "Exploring the latest drone technology for commercial, industrial and military drone uses," *businessinsider.com*, 13 July 2017, <http://www.businessinsider.com/drone-technology-uses-2017-7>.
- Mogg, T., (2017). "Drones are helping French traffic cops catch hundreds of dangerous drivers," *digitaltrends.com*, 14 November 2017, <https://www.digitaltrends.com/cool-tech/drones-help-french-traffic-cops/>.
- Reid, D. (2016). "Domino's delivers world's first ever pizza by drone," *CNBC.com*, 16 November 2016, <https://www.cnbc.com/2016/11/16/dominos-has-delivered-the-worlds-first-ever-pizza-by-drone-to-a-new-zealand-couple.html>.
- Reid, D. (2018). "A swarm of armed drones attacked a Russian military base in Syria," *CNBC.com*, 11 January 2018, <https://www.cnbc.com/2018/01/11/swarm-of-armed-diy-drones-attacks-russian-military-base-in-syria.html>.
- Sifton, J., (2012) "A Brief History of Drones," *The Nation*, 7 February 2012, <https://www.thenation.com/article/brief-history-drones/>.
- "UAV-related Events," *Wikipedia.org*, <https://en.wikipedia.org/wiki/UAV-related_events>.
- "Unmanned Aerial Vehicle," *Wikipedia.org*, <https://en.wikipedia.org/wiki/Unmanned_aerial_vehicle>.

Chapter 8   Forever Young – The Quest for Eternal Youth

- "Biological immortality," *Wikipedia.org*, <https://en.wikipedia.org/wiki/Biological_immortality>.
- Cave, S. (2012). *Immortality: The Quest To Live Forever and How It Drives Civilization*, Crown: New York.
- Global Health Observatory (GHO) (2017). *World Health Statistics 2016: Monitoring health for the SDGs*, World Health Organization (WHO): Geneva. WHO region and globally
- Grau C. et al. (2014). Conscious Brain-to-Brain Communication in Humans Using Non-Invasive Technologies. *PLOS ONE 9*(8): e105225, doi.org/10.1371/journal.pone.0105225.
- Guidi, N. et al. (2017). Osteopontin attenuates aging‐associated phenotypes of hematopoietic stem cells, *The EMBO Journal*, *36*, pp.840-853.
- Hamzelou, J. (2016). Blood from human teens rejuvenates body and brains of old mice, *New Scientist*, *3100*, 19 November 2016.
- Hamzelou, J. (2017). Antibody can protect brains from the ageing effects of old blood, *New Scientist*, *3109*, 21 January 2017.
- Hamzelou, J. (2017). Old blood can be made young again and it might fight ageing, *New Scientist*, *3118*, 25 March 2017.
- "List of longest-living organisms," *Wikipedia.org*, <https://en.wikipedia.org/wiki/List_of_longest-living_organisms>.
- Mattison, J. A. et al. (2017). Caloric restriction improves health and survival of rhesus monkeys. *Nature Communications, 8*:14063, doi: 10.1038/ncomms14063.
- "Oldest People," *Wikipedia.org*, <https://en.wikipedia.org/wiki/Oldest_people>.
- "Qin Shi Huang," *Wikipedia.org*, <https://en.wikipedia.org/wiki/Qin_Shi_Huang#Elixir_of_life>.
- Ramirez, S. et al. (2013). Creating a false memory in the hippocampus. *Science, 341*(6144), pp. 387-391.
- Sandars, N. K. (1960). *The Epic of Gilgamesh*, Peguin: London.
- Wilson, C. (2017). Calorie restriction diet extends life of monkeys by years, *New Scientist*, *3109*, 21 January 2017.
- "Turritopsis dohrnii," *Wikipedia.org*, <https://en.wikipedia.org/wiki/Turritopsis_dohrnii>.
- "Xu Fu," *Wikipedia.org*, <https://en.wikipedia.org/wiki/Xu_Fu>.

Chapter 9   Just Forget It! – The Science of Rewriting Memories

- Bellos, A. "He ate all the pi: Japanese man memorises π to 111,700 digits," *The Guardian,* 13 March 2015, <https://www.theguardian.com/science/alexs-adventures-in-numberland/2015/mar/13/pi-day-2015-memory-memorisation-world-record-japanese-akira-haraguchi>.
- Braun, K. A., Ellis, R., & Loftus, E. F. (2002). Make my memory: How advertising can change our memories of the past, *Psychology & Marketing, 19*(1), pp.1-23.
- Engelhardt, L. (1999). The problem with eyewitness testimony, *Stanford Journal of Legal Studies, 1*(1), pp.25-29.
- Hamzelou, J. (2016). Napping before an exam is as good for your memory as cramming, *New Scientist, 3100,* 19 November 2016.
- Loftus, E. F. et al. (2013). *Eyewitness Testimony: Civil and Criminal*, LexisNexis: New York.
- Phillips, H. (2017). Spotless mind: Manipulating the brain to rewrite memories, *New Scientist, 3111,* 4 February 2017.
- "Posttraumatic stress disorder," *Wikipedia.org*, <https://en.wikipedia.org/wiki/Posttraumatic_stress_disorder>.
- Ramirez, S. et al. (2013). Creating a false memory in the hippocampus. *Science, 341*(6144), pp. 387-391.
- Skeem, J. L. et al. (2009). *Psychological Science in the Courtroom, Consensus and Controversy*, The Guilford Press: New York.
- Specter, M. (2014). "Partial Recall: Can neuroscience help us rewrite our most traumatic memories?", *The New Yorker*, 19 May 2014, <https://www.newyorker.com/magazine/2014/05/19/partial-recall>.
- *The Innocence Project* <https://www.innocenceproject.org/>.
- Wise, R. A. & Safer, M. A. (2012). A Method for Analyzing the Accuracy of Eyewitness Testimony in Criminal Cases, *Court Review: The Journal of the American Judges Association, 48*, pp.22-34.

Chapter 10   I Am Who I Am – Sex, Sexuality, and Gender

- Blackless, M. et al. (2000). How sexually dimorphic are we? Review and synthesis. *American Journal of Human Biology, 12* (2), pp.151-166.
- Grabowska, A. (2017). Sex on the brain: Are gender ‑ dependent structural and functional differences associated with behavior?, *Journal of Neuroscience Research*, *95*(1-2), pp.200-212.
- Hamzelou, J. (2017). Stop multiple miscarriages, *New Scientist, 3113*, pp.8.
- Hyde, J. S. (2016). Sex and cognition: gender and cognitive functions, *Current opinion in neurobiology, 38*, pp.53-56.
- Imperato-McGinley, J., Peterson, R. E., Gautier, T. & Sturla, E. (1979). Androgens and the evolution of male-gender identity among male pseudohermaphrodites with 5α-Reductase deficiency, *New England Journal of Medicine, 300*, pp.1233-1237.
- Poiani, A. (2010). *Animal homosexuality: A Biosocial perspective,* Cambridge University Press: Cambridge.
- Swaab, D. F. (2008). Sexual orientation and its basis in brain structure and function, *PNAS, 105*(30), pp.10273-10274.
- Zhou, J. N., Hofman, M. A., Gooren, L. J., & Swaab, D. F. (1995). A sex difference in the human brain and its relation to transsexuality. *Nature, 378*, pp.68-70.
- Zietsch, B. P., et al. (2008). Genetic factors predisposing to homosexuality may increase mating success in heterosexuals, *Evolution and Human Behavior, 29*, pp.424-433.

Chapter 11   Uber, Airbnb, and TaskRabbit
– Collaborative Consumption and the Sharing Economy

- Airbnb, <https://www.airbnb.com/>.
- Airbnb Newsroom, <https://press.atairbnb.com>.
- Botsman, R., (2015). "Defining the sharing economy: what is collaborative consumption and what isn't," *fastcompany.com*, 27 May 2015, <https://www.fastcompany.com/3046119/defining-the-sharing-economy-what-is-collaborative-consumption-and-what-isnt>.
- Davidson, L., (2015). "Mapped: how the sharing economy is sweeping the world," *The Telegraph*, 23 September 2015, <https://www.telegraph.co.uk/finance/newsbysector/mediatechnologyandtelecoms/11882122/Mapped-how-the-sharing-economy-is-sweeping-the-world.html>.

- Morris, H., (2017). "The world's most prolific Airbnb owner has 881 properties in London and earns £11.9m a year," *The Telegraph*, 9 November 2017, < https://www.telegraph.co.uk/travel/news/airbnb-top-earnings-cities-landlords/>.
- "Sharing economy," *Wikipedia.org*, <https://en.wikipedia.org/wiki/Sharing_economy>.
- TaskRabbit, <https://www.taskrabbit.co.uk>.
- Uber, <https://www.uber.com/en-JP/>.
- Walker, P., (2018). "Introducing the Airbnb of car hire – would you trust a stranger with your vehicle?," *The Telegraph*, 16 March 2018, <https://www.telegraph.co.uk/travel/news/introducing-the-airbnb-of-cars/>.
- World Economic Forum, (2017), "Collaboration in Cities: From Sharing to 'Sharing Economy'," *World Economic Forum*, < http://www3.weforum.org/docs/White_Paper_Collaboration_in_Cities_report_2017.pdf>.
- Wynkoop, J., (2018). "Airbnb in Japan Local Governments Slap Strict Restrictions on Rentals,"*realestate.co.jp*, 13 December 2017, <https://resources.realestate.co.jp/news/airbnb-in-japan-local-governments-slap-strict-restrictions-on-rentals/>.

Chapter 12   More Than eMoney – What Is the Blockchain?

- Althauser, J. (2017). "Pentagon thinks blockchain technology can be used as cybersecurity shield," *Cointelegraph*, 20 August 2017, <https://cointelegraph.com/news/pentagon-thinks-blockchain-technology-can-be-used-as-cybersecurity-shield>.
- Barzilay, O. (2017). "3 ways blockchain is revolutionizing cybersecurity," *Forbes,* 21 August 2017 <https://www.forbes.com/sites/omribarzilay/2017/08/21/3-ways-blockchain-is-revolutionizing-cybersecurity/#36f122a12334>.
- Catalini, C., How Blockchain Applications Will Move Beyond Finance, T*he Harvard Business Review*, 2 March 2017.
- Cheng, E. (2018). "Japanese cryptocurrency exchange loses more than $500 million to hackers," *CNBC.com*, 26 January 2018, <https://www.cnbc.com/2018/01/26/japanese-cryptocurrency-exchange-loses-more-than-500-million-to-hackers.html>.
- Cointelegraph, (2018) "New Ethereum-Based Platform to Improve Governance Services," *Cointelegraph.com,* 26 Jan 2018, <https://cointelegraph.com/news/new-ethereum-based-platform-to-improve-governance-services>.
- Ethereum.org, <https://www.ethereum.org/>.
- Gupta, V. (2017). A Brief History of Blockchain, *The Harvard Business Review*, 28 February 2017.
- Iansiti, M., and Lakhani, K.R., The Truth About Blockchain, *The Harvard Business Review*, January to February 2017.
- Joshi, D. (2017). "As financial institutions invest in blockchain tech, how secure is your information?" *Business Insider,* 18 October 2017 <http://www.businessinsider.com/secure-cryptocurrency-blockchain-technology-2017-10>.
- McMillan, R. (2018). "The inside story of Mt. Gox, Bitcoin's $460 million disaster," *Wired*, 3 March 2014, < https://www.wired.com/2014/03/bitcoin-exchange/>.
- Ozelli, S.,(2018). "Smart Contracts Are Taking Over Functions of Lawyers: Expert Blog," *Cointelegraph.com*, < https://cointelegraph.com/news/smart-contracts-are-taking-over-functions-of-lawyers-expert-blog>. TrustToken <https://www.trusttoken.com/>.
- Wood, A. (2018). "Chinese retail giant to use blockchain to track beef, prove food safety," *Cointelegraph*, 4 March 2018, < https://cointelegraph.com/news/chinese-retail-giant-to-use-blockchain-to-track-beef-prove-food-safety>.

Chapter 13   Permanently Part-Time – Is the Gig Economy the Future of Work?

- Airbnb, <https://www.airbnb.com/>.
- Bailey, M. N. & Bosworth, B. P. (2014). US manufacturing: Understanding its past and its potential future, *Journal of Economic Perspectives, 28*(1), pp.3-26.
- "Basic income," *Wikipedia.org*, <https://en.wikipedia.org/wiki/Basic_income>.
- BBC News. (2016). "Switzerland's voters reject basic income plan," BBC News, 5 June 2016, <http://www.bbc.com/news/world-europe-36454060>.
- Bloomberg (2014). "Japanese job market shifts to part time, lower pay," *Bloomberg Visual Data,* 30 May 2014, <https://www.bloomberg.com/graphics/infographics/japanese-job-market-shifts-to-part-time.html>.
- Collantes, F. (2009). Rural Europe reshaped: the economic transformation of upland regions,

1850-2000, *Economic History Review*, *62*(2), pp.306-323.

- Collyer, B. (2017). Can we count on utopian dreamers to change the world? *New Scientist*, *3131*, 27 June 2017.
- Dogtiev, A. "Uber revenue and usage statistics 2017," *BusinessofApps*, 22 September 2017, <http://www.businessofapps.com/data/uber-statistics/>.
- Etsy, <https://www.etsy.com/uk/>.
- Gaston, N. & Kishi, T. (2007). Part-time Workers Doing Full-time Work in Japan, *Journal of the Japanese and International Economies*, *21*(4), pp.435-454.
- Hodson, H. (2016). What happens if we pay everyone just to live? *New Scientist*, *3079*, 25 June 2016.
- Kokalitcheva, K. "Uber now has 40 million monthly riders worldwide," *Fortune*, 19 October 2016, <http://fortune.com/2016/10/20/uber-app-riders/>.
- Murray, P. & Gillibrand, K. (2015). *Contingent workforce: Size, characteristics, earnings, and benefits*, U.S. Government Accountability Office: Washington D.C.
- OECD (2017). Part-time employment rate (indicator), *OECD Data*, <https://data.oecd.org/emp/part-time-employment-rate.htm>.
- Saito, O. & Shaw, L. (eds.) (2017). *Occupational structure and industrialization in a comparative perspective*, Cambridge University Press: Cambridge.
- Paine, T. (2010). *Agrarian Justice*, Wildside Press: Maryland.
- "Sharing economy," *Wikipedia.org*, <https://en.wikipedia.org/wiki/Sharing_economy>.
- Sundararajan, A. "The 'gig economy' is coming. What will it mean for work?" *The Guardian*, 26 July 2015, <https://www.theguardian.com/commentisfree/2015/jul/26/will-we-get-by-gig-economy>.
- TaskRabbit, <https://www.taskrabbit.co.uk>.
- "Temporary work," *Wikipedia.org*, <https://en.wikipedia.org/wiki/Temporary_work>.
- Trading Economics (2017). "Japan part time employment," *TradingEconomics*, 22 September 2017, <https://tradingeconomics.com/japan/part-time-employment>.
- Uber, <https://www.uber.com/en-JP/>.
- The World Factbook, *Central Intelligence Agency*, <https://www.cia.gov/library/publications/the-world-factbook/>.
- Wyatt, I. D. & Hecker, D. E. (2006). Occupational changes during the 20th century, *Monthly Labor Review*, March 2006, pp.35-57.

Chapter 14   Driven to Succeed – The Amazing Story of Elon Musk

- Carr, A., (2017), "The Real Story Behind Elon Musk's $2.6 Billion Acquisition Of SolarCity And What It Means For Tesla's Future–Not To Mention The Planet's," *fastcompany.com*, 7 June 2017, <https://www.fastcompany.com/40422076/the-real-story-behind-elon-musks-2-6-billion-acquisition-of-solarcity-and-what-it-means-for-teslas-future-not-to-mention-the-planets>.
- Davies, A., (2017). "Meet The Tesla Semitruck, Elon Musk's Most Electrifying Gamble Yet," *wired.com*, 16 November 2017, <https://www.wired.com/story/tesla-truck-revealed>.
- Kumparak, G. "Here's a video of Elon Musk watching the Falcon Heavy take off," *techcrunch.com*, 10 February 2018, <https://techcrunch.com/2018/02/10/heres-a-video-of-elon-musk-watching-the-falcon-heavy-take-off/>.
- Tesla, <https://www.tesla.com/>.
- SolarCity, <https://www.solarcity.com>.
- SpaceX, <http://www.spacex.com/>.
- Vance, A., Elon Musk, How the Billionaire CEO of SpaceX and Tesla is Shaping Our Future, Virgin Books 2016, Penguin, Random House 2015

Chapter 15   The Clanking Masses – Will a Robot Take Your Job?

- Carey, N., (2017). "Ford, Ekso team up for 'bionic' auto workers," *Reuters*, 10 November 2017, <https://www.reuters.com/article/us-ford-ekso-workers/ford-ekso-team-up-for-bionic-auto-workers-idUSKBN1D93B0>.
- The World Factbook, *Central Intelligence Agency*, <https://www.cia.gov/library/publications/the-world-factbook/>.
- Hern, A., (2017). "Google's Go-playing AI still undefeated with victory over world number one," *The Guardian*, 25 May 2017, <https://www.theguardian.com/technology/2017/may/25/alphago-google-ai-victory-world-go-number-one-china-ke-jie>.

- Lee, K., (2018). "Tech companies should stop pretending AI won't destroy jobs," *MIT Technology Review*, 21 February 2018, <https://www.technologyreview.com/s/610298/tech-companies-should-stop-pretending-ai-wont-destroy-jobs>.
- Panzarino, M. "Disney has begun populating its parks with autonomous, personality-driven robots"*Techcrunch.com,* Feb 8 2018, <https://techcrunch.com/2018/02/08/disney-has-begun-populating-its-parks-with-autonomous-personality-driven-robots/>.
- Schwab, K. (2016). "The Fourth Industrial Revolution: what it means, how to respond," *World Economic Forum*, 14 January 2016, <https://www.weforum.org/agenda/2016/01/the-fourth-industrial-revolution-what-it-means-and-how-to-respond>.
- Su, Y., (2017). "Alibaba's AI Fashion Consultant Helps Achieve Record-Setting Sales," *MIT Technology Review*, 13 November 2017, <https://www.technologyreview.com/s/609452/alibabas-ai-fashion-consultant-helps-achieve-record-setting-sales/>.
- Vlahos, J., (2018), "Inside the Alexa Prize," *Wired*, 27 February 2018, <https://www.wired.com/story/inside-amazon-alexa-prize>.
- Yirka, B., (2017). "Team in Japan creates most advanced humanoid robot yet," *TechXplore*, 21 December 2017, <https://techxplore.com/news/2017-12-team-japan-advanced-humanoid-robot.html>.

Chapter 16   It's None of Your Business! – Why Privacy Is Important
- "An Englishman's home is his castle," *Phrases.org*, <https://www.phrases.org.uk/meanings/an-englishmans-home-is-his-castle.html>.
- "Article 8: Respect for your private and family life," *Equality and Human Rights Commission*, <https://www.equalityhumanrights.com/en/human-rights-act/article-8-respect-your-private-and-family-life>.
- BBC News. (2018). "Leicester council sent care children list to taxi firms," BBC News, 12 January 2018, <http://www.bbc.com/news/uk-england-leicestershire-42667451>.
- BBC News. (2018). "Toby Young resigns from university regulator," BBC News, 9 January 2018, <http://www.bbc.com/news/uk-42617922>.
- Broomfield, M. (2016). "Teenage cyberbullying victim mocked on Facebook days after suicide in front of parents," *The Independent*, 14 December 2016, <http://www.independent.co.uk/news/world/americas/facebook-cyberbullying-victim-rebecca-ann-sedwick-after-suicide-fake-profiles-florida-a7473606.html>.
- "The Constitution of the United States," *constitutionus.com*, <http://constitutionus.com/>.
- Kumar, M. (2018). "India probes report on breach of national identity database" Reuters, 4 January 2018, <https://www.reuters.com/article/us-india-economy-biometric/india-probes-report-on-breach-of-national-identity-database-idUSKBN1ET1IX>.
- United Nations. (1948). *The Universal Declaration of Human Rights*. United Nations: New York.
- "Right to privacy," *Wikipedia.org*, <https://en.wikipedia.org/wiki/Right_to_privacy>.

Chapter 17   I'll See You in Court! – What Is the Rule of Law?
- Amnesty International. (2016). *Death Sentences and Executions 2015*, Amnesty International: London.
- Amnesty International. (2007). *When the state kills…The death penalty v. human rights*, Amnesty International: London.
- BBC News. (2016). "Mexico dismantles 'luxury cells' in Topo Chico riot jail," BBC News, 15 February 2016, <http://www.bbc.com/news/world-latin-america-35578390>.
- Benner, L. A. (2011). Eliminating excessive public defender workloads, *Criminal Justice*, *26*(2), pp.24-33.
- Death Penalty Information Center. (2016). *The death penalty in 2016: Year end report*, Death Penalty Information Center: Washington, DC.
- Pressly, L. (2016). "Cheran: The town that threw out police, politicians and gangsters," BBC News, 16 October 2016, <http://www.bbc.com/news/magazine-37612083>.
- Van Brunt, A. "Poor people rely on public defenders who are too overworked to defend them," *The Guardian,* 17 June 2015, <https://www.theguardian.com/commentisfree/2015/jun/17/poor-rely-public-defenders-too-overworked>.
- World Justice Project (2016). *Rule of Law Index 2016,* World Justice Project: Washington, DC.

Chapter 18   Just a Face in the Crowd? – What Does Social Equality Really Mean?

- Huang, J. & Russel, K. (2017). "The Highest-Paid C.E.O.s in 2016," *The New York Times*, 26 May 2017, <https://www.nytimes.com/interactive/2017/05/26/business/highest-paid-ceos.html>.
- Kochanek, K.D., Arias, E., & Anderson, R.N. (2015). Leading causes of death contributing to decrease in life expectancy gap between black and white populations: United States, 1999–2013. *NCHS data brief, 218*, National Center for Health Statistics: Hyattsville, MD.
- Mie, A. (2016). "Japanese politics a man's world as few females stand in 2016 Upper House election," *The Japan Times*, 5 July 2016, <https://www.japantimes.co.jp/news/2016/07/05/national/politics-diplomacy/japanese-politics-mans-world-females-stand-2016-upper-house-election/#.Wlg-16iWaUk>.
- Jiji. (2017). "Women hold just 3.4% of exec positions at listed Japan firms, far from 30% target: survey," *The Japan Times*, 17 January 2017, <https://www.japantimes.co.jp/news/2017/01/17/business/women-hold-just-3-4-of-exec-positions-at-listed-japan-firms-far-from-30-target-survey/#.Wlg-5KiWaUk>.
- United Nations. (1948). *The Universal Declaration of Human Rights*. United Nations: New York.
- United Nations. (2017). *World Economic Situation and Prospects 2018*. United Nations Department of Economic and Social Affairs: New York
- "Facts and figures: Leadership and political participation," *UN Women*, <http://www.unwomen.org/en/what-we-do/leadership-and-political-participation/facts-and-figures>.
- Zarya, V. (2017). The 2017 Fortune 500 Includes a Record Number of Women CEOs, *Fortune*, 7 June 2017 <http://fortune.com/2017/06/07/fortune-women-ceos/>.

Chapter 19   Freedom of the Press Means Freedom of the People
– The Danger of Fake News

- Hern, A., (2017). "Thirty countries use 'armies of opinion shapers' to manipulate democracy – report," *The Guardian*, 14 November 2017, <https://www.theguardian.com/technology/2017/nov/14/social-media-influence-election-countries-armies-of-opinion-shapers-manipulate-democracy-fake-news>.
- Kirby, E. (2016) "The city getting rich from fake news," BBC News, 5 December 2016, <http://www.bbc.com/news/magazine-38168281>.
- Kleinman, Z., (2018). "Fake news 'travels faster', study finds,"BBC News, 9 March 2018, <http://www.bbc.com/news/technology-43344256>.
- The Onion, <https://www.theonion.com/>.
- Schaedel, S., "Did the Pope Endorse Trump?," *Factcheck.org*, 24 October 2016, <https://www.factcheck.org/2016/10/did-the-pope-endorse-trump>.
- Silverman, C., (2016) "This Analysis Shows How Viral Fake Election News Stories Outperformed Real News On Facebook," *Buzzfeed News*, 17 November 2016, <https://www.buzzfeed.com/craigsilverman/viral-fake-election-news-outperformed-real-news-on-facebook?utm_term=.fyklpzZGQY#.ukvO3rbG1A>.
- Subramanian, S., "Inside The Macedonian Fake News Complex,"*Wired*, 15 February 2017, <https://www.wired.com/2017/02/veles-macedonia-fake-news>.
- Titcomb, J. and Carson, J., (2018). "Fake news: What exactly is it – and how can you spot it?,"*The Telegraph*, 19 March 2018, <https://www.telegraph.co.uk/technology/0/fake-news-exactly-has-really-had-influence>.

Chapter 20   One in a Million – Why Your Vote Counts

- BBC News. (2017). "Virginia Democrat Shelly Simonds 'takes seat by one vote'," BBC News, 20 December 2017, <http://www.bbc.com/news/world-us-canada-42426404>.
- Desilver, D. (2017). "U.S. trails most developed countries in voter turnout," *Pew Research Center*, <http://www.pewresearch.org/fact-tank/2017/05/15/u-s-voter-turnout-trails-most-developed-countries/>.
- The Economist Intelligence Unit. (2017). *Democracy Index 2016*. The Economist Intelligence Unit: London.
- "National Rifle Association," *Wikipedia.org*, <https://en.wikipedia.org/wiki/National_Rifle_Association>.
- "Population," *United States Census Bureau*, <https://census.gov/topics/population.html>.
- "Voting Turnout Statistics," *Statistic Brain*, <https://www.statisticbrain.com/voting-statistics/>.

TEXT PRODUCTION STAFF

edited by 編集
Kimio Sato 佐藤 公雄

English-language editing by 英文校閲
Bill Benfield ビル・ベンフィールド

cover design by 表紙デザイン
Ruben Frosali ルーベン・フロサリ

text design by 本文デザイン
Ruben Frosali ルーベン・フロサリ

CD PRODUCTION STAFF

narrated by 吹き込み者
Hannah Grace (AmerE) ハンナ・グレース（アメリカ英語）
Bob Werley (AmerE) ボブ・ワーリー（アメリカ英語）

World of Wonders: A Brave New World
知の探索

2019年1月20日　初版発行
2023年4月10日　第6刷発行

編著者　Anthony Sellick
　　　　John Barton
　　　　小笠原 亜衣

発行者　佐野 英一郎
発行所　株式会社 成美堂
　　　　〒101-0052　東京都千代田区神田小川町3-22
　　　　TEL 03-3291-2261　FAX 03-3293-5490
　　　　https://www.seibido.co.jp

印刷・製本　倉敷印刷(株)

ISBN 978-4-7919-7191-6　　　　　　　　　　　　　Printed in Japan

・落丁・乱丁本はお取り替えします。
・本書の無断複写は、著作権上の例外を除き著作権侵害となります。